GOLDEN HOMEMAKERS

101 Delicious dishes for summer cooking

Marshall Cavendish London & New York

Introduction

Summer is the natural time to liven up your approach to cooking and dining. With the wide availability of fresh foods, herbs and seasonings you can easily create many refreshingly different dishes. In this Golden Homemaker volume, we've included Pineapple Pol, Salmon Trout with Green Herb Sauce, Lamb and Apricot Kebabs to mention just a few.

Many desserts really come into their own in the summer so you can experiment with these too, perhaps just to serve at a sunny afternoon get-together. There are many to choose from including an elegant Charlotte Russe, Finnish Lemon Cake, and a tempting Gooseberry Sorbet.

We've included a special section to help you make the most of entertaining possibilities with suggestions for a distinctive buffet, an out-of-the-ordinary Smorgasbord, a fun picnic and a barbecue.

We suggest ways to get the most out of your refrigerator or freezer as well, so that you can cook up some things ahead of time and keep them fresh.

In fact, we think you'll find that you will want to use this book not just in the summer, but right through the year – whenever you want an inspirational lift for your cooking.

Contents

Cooking in the Summertime	2
Making the Most of your Refrigerator	5
Appetizers and First Courses	6
Summer Soups	10
Fish Dishes	14
Light Meals	18
Main Course Meat Dishes	22
Main Course Poultry Dishes	28
Vegetable Accompaniments	12
Salads and Salad Dressings	36
Just Desserts	40
Fresh Fruit Desserts	44
Summertime Entertaining	49
Buffet Spreads	50
Barbecue Dishes	52
A Smorrebrod Meal	54
Picnic Parties	56
Icy Thirst-Quenchers	58
Basic Recipes	61
Carving Meat and Preparing Fish	62
Glossary of Cooking Terms	63

101 Delicious Dishes for Summer Cooking was prepared for Marshall Cavendish Limited by Spectator Publications Limited © Marshall Cavendish Limited 1973, 1976

Published by
Marshall Cavendish Publications Limited
58 Old Compton Street
London W1V 5PA

ISBN   0 85685 182 5

Printed in Great Britain by
Petty and Sons Limited, Leeds.

101 DELICIOUS DISHES FOR SUMMER COOKING

COOKING IN THE SUMMERTIME

Traditionally, summertime is the season when cooks prefer to spend as little time as possible in the kitchen, and when the cooking and preparation of food in general are kept down to an absolute minimum.

Certainly, in warm weather it is more pleasant to serve dishes which may be prepared with a minimum of fuss and bother—yet this does not mean that all cookery which is in the slightest elaborate is entirely out of place. Summer holidays and vacations often mean that we have a little more time and opportunity to entertain in one way or another. Again, you need not be overly elaborate, but certainly parties of an informal nature are thoroughly seasonal (and attractive and exciting cookery is never out of season!).

Furthermore don't be led to believe that cold food is the only appropriate summertime food. Endless salads and cold platters appearing day after day in a steady succession, can do nothing to excite the appetites of the eaters. Of course, some cold dishes are delicious in summer (and at other times of the year as well), and salads can be made tasty and interesting. But a constant diet of any one dish is hardly the way to please your family or friends, or to encourage an interest and appreciation of food in general. You may have noticed that many of the countries with the hottest climates traditionally serve hot, spicy and rich foods—so merely serving cold food cannot be the answer to hot weather, especially if doing so will tend to dull rather than stimulate appetites.

Seasonal foods
We believe that one of the most important aspects of summertime cookery is imaginative use of seasonal food. Today, with the enormous advances in the storage of food which have been made, and with the wide

availability of refrigerators and freezers as well as frozen and pre-packaged foods, we are all less aware of basic restrictions on foods than were our parents.

And yet, one of the few remaining true pleasures of cooking in the summer is the use of the fresh foods which are then available: the new potatoes and peas, the first strawberries and raspberries, the juicy pineapples; the lamb; the salmon and salmon trout, the mullet and crab. What greater delight could there be than a meal which is simply composed of such luxuries, appropriately served when they are at their height of flavour and freshness?

Many foods, because of quick freezing, are available out of season—many of those mentioned in the last paragraph may be had without difficulty (though at a price) in winter as well as at the time of their greatest abundance in summer. And if you own a freezer yourself, it makes good sense to buy these foods in bulk when they are at their cheapest, and preserve some for later consumption.

Cooking with herbs

At the same time, however, it is scarcely sensible to pay inflated prices for out-of-season foods and to ignore the advantages of their use at the times when they *are* relatively cheap. And since summer provides the greatest wealth of seasonal foods, the best way of profiting from their supply is to learn to enjoy cooking them at the appropriate time. Learning to cook well with fresh and delicious foods is hardly a burden—and especially when you have the added advantage in the summertime of having an enormous variety of fresh herbs which are so much more preferable to their dried counterparts. If you have space outside to plant a

small herb garden, you will find this by far the most reliable way of obtaining the flavourings you need—or perhaps you can arrange a window box in your kitchen for those herbs which may be grown in pots. During the summer some supermarkets and the more specialist stores stock fresh herbs (over and above the usually obtainable parsley, mint and chives) and it may help to enquire about supplies of tarragon, basil, fennel, fresh bay leaves, thyme and marjoram at your local shop. The more 'cosmopolitan' your area, the more likely you are to find the more unusual herbs. If you live near a nursery it may pay to enquire there about the availability of fresh herbs, although in general it is only a small number of enthusiasts who produce them regularly.

Although tastes differ, the main herbs which you will want to use with any regularity in summer (and if you do grow your own, use fresh-dried ones at other times of the year too in preference to shop-bought ones) are the following:

Basil—a rather delicate plant to grow, which needs the protected warmth of a greenhouse or a very sunny sheltered corner. An aromatic and delicious herb; used with pasta, fish, soups, sauces, and almost all vegetable dishes.

Bay—an evergreen shrub. Used in the traditional *bouquet garni* in flavouring soups and stews, with chicken and beef, and in stuffings and pâtés.

Chives—a rather pretty plant when it produces its blue flowers. Used in all potato dishes (especially potato salad) and in many other salads as well, especially a green or tomato salad.

Marjoram—the western equivalent of the Italian *origanum* and the Greek wild *rigani*. Used in pastas and tomato based dishes, and with chicken, beef and veal.

Mint—many varieties are available and most grow well; the most usual is the spearmint. Instead of the traditional mint sauce, try using it in the Middle Eastern fashion in soups, salads (especially good with cucumber and yogurt salad) or with chicken or rice dishes.

Parsley—it makes good sense to grow a lot of this, so that some is always on hand for garnishing soups and adding to salads and sauces. It is a herb to be lavish with.

Tarragon—always make sure that you are buying French tarragon (the sort sometimes referred to as Russian tarragon has no flavour at all). The French variety has a very distinct aroma and taste, and is essential to many classic dishes. Used with chicken, fish, vegetable dishes, in Sauce Béarnaise, in a *fines herbes* omelette with chives, and in many salads.

Thyme—many varieties are available; most make very good additions to your herb range. Lemon thyme has a rather delicate flavour which is particularly good with fish and poultry dishes; and the more common varieties are excellent in stews and soups, terrines and pâtés, and with grilled meats.

MAKING THE MOST OF YOUR REFRIGERATOR

Economical advantages

A refrigerator has become one of the most important assets for the housewife who must cope with summer cooking. Few days will pass during the hot weather when it will not be possible to make use of it for storing or preserving, or helping to make or improve a dish. Recently there has been an enormous increase in the number of household food-freezers, and these offer the extra appeal of the economies that can be found in the bulk purchase of frozen goods.

With the warmer weather it is pleasant to cut down on lengthy, tiring shopping trips; and the weekly expedition which is now widely practiced can be reduced even further with careful planning over the sorts of food that can be stored in your refrigerator. Planning your menus —and making a list in advance—means that you can save time in each shop, and also avoid the extra cost of unnecessary food bought on impulse. It is most important that you should know the storage times for food to be kept in a frozen food compartment and as this varies so much depending on the size and type of each appliance be sure to follow the instructions supplied with each model.

As well as economies on frozen produce from the shops, a food freezer also offers an outlet for excess crops of fresh fruit and vegetables. During the summer your kitchen garden will be at its most productive, meaning that tiny, fresh vegetables and soft fruit can be preserved and enjoyed during the winter months, reminding one pleasantly of the summer. Again it is important to learn as much as possible about the capacity and scope of your own freezer before you start storing any produce, or else you may waste time and space preserving foods that do not freeze satisfactorily. There is

such a wide variety of fruit and vegetables that it is easy to obtain and use only those that will give the best results.

When storing anything in the refrigerator it is best to cover or wrap as much as possible because any strong-flavoured food will taint other more delicate foods. It is easy to use plastic film or foil to cover bowls or bottles; and cheese and bacon can be kept in airtight plastic boxes which prevent the produce from drying out in the cold. These boxes can also be used to keep extra pastry or 'rubbed-in' fat which can be made in large quantities when you have spare time and used when needed.

Any time that can be saved in the preparation of food means that you will be free when the weather suggests it would be nicer to spend your time out of the kitchen. In hot weather the risk of infection from flies and bacteria increases, and a refrigerator offers the perfect protection for all foods, especially dairy produce and meat. Do not wrap meat too tightly because the exclusion of air will spoil it, but keep it covered so that the exposed surfaces will not turn hard and dry.

Hints on serving chilled foods

It is wise to remember that in an effort to counteract the heat with cold refreshing food one should not necessarily serve ice-cold dishes, but simply chilled food which is much nicer to eat. Many items are improved with chilling and can be served straight from the refrigerator, but others lose much of their flavour when they are very cold—these should be stored in the refrigerator only to preserve them, and removed from it and left to reach room temperature before they are eaten. This is particularly true of cold meats and poultry—they can be carved cold

when taken from the refrigerator, and the slices left under cover to lose their chill.

Cold drinks make a most welcome treat on hot days, and a little fore-thought means a refrigerator can be a great help. Keep a jug of water in there so that really cold drinks can be served at once; freeze double-strength orange drink in the icetray and add cubes of this to your drink. If you plan summer entertaining make sure you keep bottles of white wine in your refrigerator so that there isn't a last minute panic trying to cool it once your guests have arrived.

Children are synonymous with ice-cream and water-ices during the hot weather, which can prove very costly if these items are purchased separately. Instead use one of the 'water-ice' kits and produce a variety of interesting flavours, perhaps adding fresh fruit to the mixture before freezing. Try diluting a jelly [jello] mix with half the recommended amount of water and freezing this solution in an icetray to make unusual cool desserts for the children. With a refrigerator or freezer it is possible to store large, economy packs of ice-cream, and these together with a supply of wafers or cones can halve the refreshment bill.

Many of the recipes in this book allow time for chilling or overnight refrigeration, which means that much of the preparation can be done in advance, leaving the refrigerator to complete your work. It will then simply remain for you to decorate if necessary before serving.

When most women and men have so much to do it is no longer considered lazy to take full advantage of modern convenience foods and appliances. A refrigerator or freezer must now be considered chief among these in enabling you to save time and energy and so enjoy the leisure of summer.

APPETIZERS & FIRST COURSES

Some truly delicious ways in which to tempt and whet the appetite in almost any weather! An unusual way of serving grapefruit; an intriguing addition for avocados; devilled scallops—each of these dishes is different enough from the usual way of presentation to make your meals begin (as they should) by combining interesting flavours in attractive ways—yet without introducing any heaviness which might dull the rest of the meal's enjoyment. Try the Mexican Guacamole, the traditional French Crudités, or the Italian-style Fried Whitebait to give your menu an 'international' touch.

below: Les Crudités

Fried Whitebait

Cooking and preparation time:
30 minutes
SERVES 4-6

1 lb. whitebait or small fresh sardines
2½ oz. [½ cup plus 2 tablespoons] flour
1 teaspoon salt
½ teaspoon freshly milled black
   pepper
vegetable oil for deep frying
To garnish:
parsley sprigs
lemon slices

Rinse the whitebait in cold water then drain well and dry on absorbent kitchen paper.
Put the whitebait, flour and seasoning into a large bag and shake until each fish is evenly coated with seasoned flour.
Transfer the fish to a frying basket, shaking well to remove all the surplus flour. Heat the oil for deep frying.
Fry the whitebait a few at a time in deep fat, taking care to shake the frying basket frequently to prevent the fish from sticking together. Drain each batch well on absorbent kitchen paper.
Serve garnished with parsley and lemon slices.

Melons with Mulled Wine

Preparation time:
15 minutes, plus 1 hour refrigeration time
SERVES 4

2 small melons (see Note below)
10 fl. oz. [1¼ cups] sweet red wine
slice of orange
slice of lemon
1 small stick cinnamon
pinch of allspice
2 cloves
2 teaspoons honey

Wrap the whole melons in aluminium foil and chill.
Heat the wine with the fruit, spices and honey and simmer for 10-15 minutes. Strain and chill well.
Cut the melons in half and scoop out the seeds.

Place each half in a shallow fruit dish. If the melon is too large to fit a dish, cut a very thin slice from each base so that the melon will stand firmly on a plate.
Spoon the chilled wine mixture into the melons just before serving. If preferred, this dish may be served as a dessert.

Note: For melons with mulled wine, the more unusual Charantais or Ogen melons are the nicest, although Honeydew or Canteloupe may be used. All these melons can be used in a variety of ways as first courses. Do not put melons of any sort in the refrigerator unless they are well-wrapped because the flavour will affect other foods, especially milk and cream.

Variations:
§ Cut the melon flesh into cubes and mix with segments of orange in small glass dishes, sprinkle with French dressing and serve chilled.
§ Serve thick slices of melon with powdered ginger and soft brown sugar.
§ Serve the slices of melon with Parma ham.
§ Cut the melon in half, discard the seeds and scrape out the flesh with a Parisienne or ball cutter. Mix the flesh with a few raspberries and strawberries in small glass bowls, and sprinkle with sugar and lemon juice or a little liqueur or sweet sherry.

Peppermint Ice Grapefruit

Preparation time:
30 minutes, plus 1-2 hours refrigeration time
SERVES 4

1 egg white
2 oz. castor [¼ cup fine] sugar
4 grapefruit
4-8 teaspoons Crème de Menthe

Place the egg white in a small plate or saucer. Dip the rims of 4 serving glasses in the egg white and then in the castor [fine] sugar. Stand the glasses upright and set aside for about 1 hour until the egg white and sugar harden and form an attractive rim.
Meanwhile, using a sharp knife, remove and discard the zest and white pith from each grapefruit. Cut out each segment of grapefruit, leaving behind

the pith. This is best done over a bowl to catch the juice.
Carefully fill the prepared glasses with the grapefruit segments and juice.
Add 1-2 teaspoons of Crème de Menthe to each glass.
Chill for 1-2 hours before serving.

Guacamole

Avocado Pâté

Preparation time:
10 minutes plus 30 minutes refrigeration time
SERVES 4

1 shallot
1 large or 2 small avocados
2 tablespoons sour cream
1 tablespoon lemon juice
⅛ teaspoon salt
pinch white pepper

Peel the shallot and grate finely into a bowl. Press the shallot with the back of a spoon to extract as much juice as possible. Reserve the juice and discard the shallot.
Peel the avocado, discard the stone and pound the flesh in a mortar with a pestle, or liquidise in an electric blender until reduced to a pulp. Add the onion juice, sour cream, lemon juice, salt and pepper and beat until well-blended. Chill well.
Serve the guacamole in small amounts on individual plates, with brown bread and butter, or melba toast.

Pineapple Pol

Preparation time:
30 minutes, plus 1 hour refrigeration time
SERVES 4

2 small ripe pineapples
½ small cucumber
¼ small honeydew melon
Roquefort Dressing (see page 38)

Cut each pineapple in half lengthwise, through the green spikes.
Cut out the pineapple flesh and chop it coarsely. Dice the cucumber and the melon flesh or, if you have a melon or Parisienne cutter, scoop the melon out in little balls.
Pile the prepared fruit into each

pineapple half and chill well.
Dress with a little Roquefort Dressing just before serving or with plain French Dressing (see page 38).

Baked Avocado with Crab

 ① ① ① ▨

Preparation and cooking time:
35 minutes
SERVES 4

1 shallot
12 oz. frozen or canned white crabmeat with cartilage removed
10 fl. oz. [1¼ cups] Béchamel sauce (see page 61)
1 tablespoon tomato purée
2 tablespoons lemon juice
1 oz. [2 tablespoons] butter
2 avocados
To garnish:
1 teaspoon chopped parsley
½ teaspoon paprika

Heat the oven to 375°F (Gas Mark 5, 190°C).
Peel and finely chop the shallot and mix it in a small saucepan with the crabmeat, Béchamel sauce, tomato purée and lemon juice. Warm through slowly over low heat.
Halve the avocados and remove the stones.
Pile the crabmeat mixture into the cavity of each avocado half and place them in an ovenproof dish. Pour a little water around the avocados and cover with a lid or with aluminium foil.
Place on the top shelf of the preheated oven and bake for 15 minutes.
Sprinkle with parsley and paprika just before serving.

Les Crudités

 ① ① ▨

Preparation time:
45 minutes
SERVES 4

Les Crudités can be found on nearly every restaurant menu in France—from the humblest to the most sophisticated. The dish is a mixture of raw vegetables, prepared with various dressings and sauces, and served as an appetizer or hors d'oeuvres. The choice of vegetables will depend on what is available and on individual

taste, but here is a typical selection of vegetables and dressings to serve.

4 large firm tomatoes
½ small cucumber
4 tablespoons French Dressing
chopped parsley
4 medium-sized carrots
1 shallot
6 tablespoons Tarragon Dressing
8 stalks of celery
1 head chicory [endive]
1 tablespoon lemon juice
1 tablespoon olive oil

Thinly slice the tomatoes and cucumber and arrange them in small separate dishes. Sprinkle with French Dressing and chopped parsley.
Peel and grate the carrots and shallot and mix them with a little Tarragon Dressing. Arrange this in another dish.
Cut the celery and chicory into fine strips and dress with lemon juice and olive oil. Arrange them in a serving dish. If preferred all the vegetables can be placed together in a large bowl, and the sauces served separately.
The vegetables are often served with Mayonnaise and rich sauces such as Rémoulade sauce (see page 62). They may also be served with sardines, tuna fish, coeur de palmier or artichoke hearts and a slice of ham, pâté or salami.

Moules au Gratin

Grilled mussels with breadcrumbs

 ① ① ▨

Preparation and cooking time:
35 minutes
SERVES 4

1 quart [2½ pints] mussels
1 shallot
8 fl. oz. [1 cup] dry white wine
½ teaspoon salt
¼ teaspoon pepper
3-4 sprigs parsley
1 bay leaf
1½ oz. [3 tablespoons] butter
3 oz. [1½ cup] fine fresh breadcrumbs

Heat the grill [broiler] at its highest setting.
Scrub the mussels very thoroughly under cold running water and remove the beards. Discard any mussels which are not tightly closed, as they are not fit to eat. Peel and chop the shallot.
Put the mussels in a large saucepan and add the shallot, wine, salt, pepper,

parsley and bay leaf. Cover tightly.
Heat over a high flame for 8-10 minutes or until the mussels have opened. Any mussels which do not open must be discarded.
Take the mussels out of the saucepan and remove one shell from each. Place the mussels on their remaining shells in a shallow ovenproof dish. Sprinkle with the breadcrumbs and put a dot of butter on each mussel. Grill [broil] for 3-4 minutes until the breadcrumbs are crisp and golden brown.
Serve immediately.

Devilled Scallops

 ① ① ▨

Preparation and cooking time:
35 minutes
SERVES 4

8 scallops
1 shallot
1 clove of garlic
10 fl. oz. [1¼ cups] milk
1 oz. [2 tablespoons] butter
2 tablespoons flour
½ level teaspoon curry powder
1 tablespoon sherry
dash Tabasco sauce
4 tablespoons fine fresh breadcrumbs

Heat the grill [broiler] at its highest setting.
Remove the scallops from their shells and rinse well. Keep 4 shells for serving. Peel and finely chop the shallot and garlic.
Dice the scallops and place them in a saucepan with the milk, shallot and garlic. Bring to the boil slowly over moderate heat then lower the flame and simmer for about 10 minutes. Strain off the liquid and reserve.
Meanwhile, melt the butter in a small saucepan. Stir in the flour and curry powder; then add the reserved liquid, a little at a time. Bring to the boil, stirring continuously, until the mixture thickens.
Add the diced scallops, the sherry and Tabasco sauce, and mix well. Fill the 4 shells with the mixture and sprinkle with breadcrumbs.
Grill [broil] for 2-3 minutes until the breadcrumbs are crisp and golden brown.
Serve immediately.

opposite: top: Peppermint Ice Grapefruit, Fried Whitebait
foreground: Moules au Gratin

SUMMER SOUPS

Soup makes an ideal first course for a summer meal, where it may be the only hot dish to be served. And of course, a chilled soup can often bring a certain glamour to enhance a menu.

Many cooks today avoid serving soups—perhaps because they tend to believe they are rather uninteresting, and lacking in texture and taste appeal. These recipes prove just the opposite, with deliciously different combinations. of both usual and unusual ingredients which make dishes for very special occasions—yet many inexpensive enough to be enjoyed every day.

left: Fish and Potato Soup
below: Tomato and Orange Soup

Fish and Potato Soup

☆ ① ◫ ◫

Preparation and cooking time:
1 hour
SERVES 4-5

1½ lbs. white fish (cod, haddock or
    whiting)
1½ pints [3¾ cups] water
1 lb. new potatoes
1 shallot
2 stalks of celery
1 oz. [2 tablespoons] butter
grated zest of 1 lemon
1 bay leaf
3 tablespoons coarsely chopped
    parsley
6 fl. oz. [¾ cup] milk
freshly milled black pepper
3 teaspoons cornflour [cornstarch]
salt

Remove any skin and bone from the
fish and simmer it in the water for
about 15 minutes. Strain and reserve
the cooking liquid.
Cut the fish into 2-inch pieces. Peel
and thickly slice the potatoes. Peel
and finely chop the shallot. Thinly
slice the celery.
Heat the butter in a large saucepan
and sauté the shallot and celery for
2-3 minutes.
Add the pieces of fish and potato and
sauté for a further 5 minutes.
Add the lemon zest, bay leaf, half of
the parsley, the milk, the reserved
stock and pepper. Simmer for 20
minutes, or until the fish and potato
are tender.
Blend the cornflour [cornstarch] with a
little cold water and stir into the soup.
Bring to the boil, stirring continuously
until the mixture thickens. Season
according to taste.
Sprinkle with the remaining parsley
and serve hot.

Tomato and Orange Soup

☆ ① ① ◫ ◫

Preparation and cooking time:
1½ hours
SERVES 4-6

1½ lb. tomatoes
1 large onion
1 carrot

grated zest of 1 lemon
1 bay leaf
4 peppercorns
1½ pints [3¾ cups] chicken stock
1 orange
1½ oz. [3 tablespoons] butter
4 tablespoons flour
6 fl. oz. single [¾ cup light] cream

Coarsely chop the tomatoes, onion and
carrot, and place them in a large
saucepan with the lemon zest, bay leaf,
peppercorns and chicken stock. Bring
to the boil then lower the heat and
simmer for 1 hour.
Meanwhile, finely shred the orange
zest. Blanch in boiling water and
drain. Squeeze out the orange juice.
Remove the tomato mixture from the
heat and press it through a sieve to
reduce it to a purée.
Melt the butter in a saucepan and
stir in the flour. Add the sieved
mixture and stir until well-blended.
Bring to the boil, stirring continuously
until the mixture thickens.
Remove from the heat and stir in the
orange juice and zest.
Pour into individual bowls, and add a
little cream to each one.

Curried Shellfish Soup

☆ ① ① ◫

Preparation and cooking time:
25 minutes
SERVES 4-6

3 stalks of celery
1½ oz. [3 tablespoons] butter
4 tablespoons flour
2 teaspoons curry powder
1½ pints [3¾ cups] chicken stock
4-inch piece cucumber, diced
4-6 oz. shrimps or prawns, shelled
2 teaspoons grated lemon zest
2 tablespoons medium sweet sherry
To garnish:
1 tablespoon chopped parsley

Thinly slice the celery. Melt the butter
in a large saucepan and sauté the
celery for 5 minutes, without letting
it brown.
Stir in the flour and curry powder,
then add the stock a little at a time.
Bring the mixture to the boil, stirring
continuously until it thickens.
Add the cucumber together with the
prawns or shrimps, lemon zest and
sherry. Heat for 2-3 minutes.
Pour the soup into a large bowl and

sprinkle with chopped parsley before
serving.

Cream of Cucumber Soup

☆ ① ◫ ◫

Preparation and cooking time:
1 hour
SERVES 4-6

1 large cucumber
2 tablespoons chopped chives
2 tablespoons chopped parsley
16 fl. oz. [2 cups] water
16 fl. oz. [2 cups] milk
1 teaspoon salt
¼ teaspoon freshly milled white
    pepper
2 tablespoons cornflour [cornstarch]
4-6 tablespoons double [heavy]
    cream

Grate the cucumber into a saucepan
and add the chives, parsley, water,
10 fl. oz. [1¼ cups] of the milk, and
the salt and pepper. Bring to the boil
then lower the heat and simmer for
35-40 minutes.
Press the mixture through a sieve or
reduce to a purée in a blender.
Blend the cornflour [cornstarch] with
the remaining milk and stir into the
soup. Return to the heat and bring to
the boil, stirring continuously until
the soup thickens.
Taste the soup and add more salt and
pepper, if necessary.
Serve hot or cold with a little cream
added.

Vichyssoise

☆ ① ◫ ◫

Preparation and cooking time:
1½ hours
SERVES 5-6

1½ lbs. floury potatoes
4 large leeks
1 large onion
3-4 sprigs parsley
1½ pints [3¾ cups] chicken stock
6 fl. oz. [¾ cup] milk
salt and pepper
To garnish
2 tablespoons chopped chives
6 fl. oz. single [¾ cup light] cream

Peel and dice the potatoes. Trim off
the root end of the leeks and the very

tough green parts. Separate the layers of leek and rinse well under cold running water. Cut into small pieces. Peel and chop the onion.

Place the potato, leek, onion, parsley, chicken stock and milk in a large saucepan. Bring to the boil, then lower the heat and simmer for 1 hour.

Press the mixture through a sieve to reduce to a purée. Season the purée with salt and pepper and stir in a little extra milk to thin down the soup, if necessary.

If the vichyssoise is to be served hot, pour into individual bowls, add a . little cream to each one and sprinkle with chopped chives.

If it is to be served cold, chill well and then thin down with milk, if necessary. Garnish with chives and cream before serving.

Chilled Fruit Soup

Preparation and cooking time:
1 hour plus 1-2 hours refrigeration time
SERVES 4-6

1 eating apple
1 pear
1 peach
3 plums
3 apricots
1 small cinnamon stick
3 cloves
1½ pints [3¾ cups] water or a mixture of white wine and water
1 teaspoon chopped crystallized [candied] ginger
4 oz. raspberries
4 oz. strawberries
1 tablespoon cornflour [cornstarch]
3 tablespoons lemon juice
10 fl. oz. [1¼ cups] fresh or canned orange juice
castor [fine] sugar

Peel, core and dice the apple and pear. Peel, stone and dice the peach, plums and apricots.

Tie the cinnamon and cloves in a small piece of muslin. Put the prepared fruit in a large saucepan with the spices, liquid and ginger.

Bring to the boil then lower the heat and simmer for 20-30 minutes or until the fruits are soft. Remove the cinnamon and cloves. Rinse the raspberries and strawberries and add to the other fruit, simmering for a further 10 minutes.

Blend the cornflour [cornstarch] with the lemon juice and stir into the soup. When the mixture thickens slightly, remove from the heat and set aside to cool, stirring occasionally.

Stir in the orange juice and add sugar to taste.

Chill well before serving.

Onion Consommé

Preparation and cooking time:
1 hour
SERVES 4

1 lb. onions
2 cloves of garlic
2 tablespoons vegetable oil
1½ pints [3¾ cups] chicken stock
1 bay leaf
salt and pepper
1 egg white and egg shell, crushed
2 tablespoons sherry
To garnish:
1 shallot, thinly sliced and divided into rings

Peel and chop the onion and garlic and place them in a saucepan. Heat the oil and sauté the onion and garlic until soft and just beginning to brown.

Add the chicken stock and bay leaf and bring to the boil. Lower the heat and simmer for 30 minutes. Season to taste with salt and pepper and set aside to cool a little.

Drop the egg white and egg shell into the saucepan and whisk over low heat until the surface becomes very frothy.

Increase the heat and just as the froth rises to the top of the pan, draw the pan off the heat. Strain into a bowl through a jelly bag or a piece of fine muslin in a sieve. Stir in the sherry. Chill well.

Pour the consommé into small bowls and garnish with shallot.

Yogurt and Vegetable Soup

Preparation time:
45 minutes plus 1-2 hours refrigeration time
SERVES 4-6

12 oz. pickled beetroots [beets]
½ small cucumber

2 radishes
2 shallots
2 cloves of garlic
1 pint [2½ cups] natural yogurt
1 pint [2½ cups] cold chicken stock
4-6 oz. prawns or shrimps, shelled
2 hard-boiled eggs
salt
pepper
sugar
1 tablespoon finely chopped parsley
1 tablespoon chopped fresh dill or mint

Cut the beetroot [beet] and cucumber into fine matchsticks. Slice the radishes. Peel and finely chop the shallots and garlic.

Mix the prepared vegetables with the yogurt, chicken stock and prawns or shrimps. Chill well. Meanwhile, shell and chop the eggs.

Season the soup to taste with salt, pepper and sugar, and pour into individual bowls. Sprinkle with chopped egg, parsley and dill, and serve immediately.

Avgolemono Soup

Greek lemon and egg soup

Preparation time:
30 minutes
SERVES 4

1½ pints [3¾ cups] chicken stock (made from chicken carcass, not stock cubes)
2-3 tablespoons long-grain rice
2 eggs
3 tablespoons lemon juice
salt
¼ teaspoon white pepper

Heat the chicken stock in a large saucepan until simmering.

Rinse the rice thoroughly under cold running water and add it to the chicken stock. Simmer until the rice is tender, then remove from the heat.

Whisk the eggs with the lemon juice and add 4-5 tablespoons of the chicken stock, stirring continuously.

Whisk the lemon mixture into the stock and reheat, stirring continuously until almost boiling.

Add the seasoning and serve hot.

opposite: Curried Shellfish Soup

FISH DISHES

Fish of many varieties are here served in imaginative ways—to make each a pleasure to cook as well as to eat. These dishes are intended to be served as main courses, but you can always reduce the quantities and serve them as first courses instead—the Sole Provençale, the Marinated Herrings or the Moules Marinière would be good choices, while the Bouchées aux Fruits de Mer makes an excellent buffet party dish.

Presenting fish dishes attractively adds enormously to their appeal—red mullet, for instance, is both beautiful and delicious when cooked, as in the recipe here, with fennel and wine.

below: Salmon Trout with Green Herb Sauce, Goujons de Sole Provençale

Moules Marinière

Seaman's mussels

Preparation and cooking time:
20 minutes
SERVES 4

2 quarts [5 pints] mussels
10 fl. oz. [1¼ cups] white wine
2 large onions
3 cloves of garlic
2 tablespoons chopped parsley

Scrub the mussels under cold running water and remove the beards. Discard any which are not tightly closed, as they are not fit to eat.
Place them in a large saucepan and add the wine, onions, garlic and parsley.
Cover tightly and place over high heat for about 5 minutes or until the mussels open. Discard any mussels which do not open.
Using a large spoon, take out the mussels and juice and place on warm serving dishes.
Serve immediately with crusty French bread and butter.

Marinated Herrings

Preparation time:
30 minutes, plus 4-5 hours marinating time
SERVES 4

4 herrings, cleaned and soaked in salt water for 1 hour
4 oz. castor [½ cup fine] sugar
8 fl. oz [1 cup] malt or cider vinegar
1 bay leaf
1 tablespoon pickling spice
To garnish:
2 tomatoes, cut into wedges
fresh dill sprigs

Heat the sugar, vinegar, bay leaf and pickling spice together to boiling point. Set aside to cool.
Drain the herrings, dry well and cut into 1-1½ inch pieces. Place in a bowl and add the vinegar mixture. Set aside to marinate for 3-4 hours.
Remove the pieces of herring from the marinade and arrange in a serving dish.
Garnish with wedges of tomato and

sprigs of fresh dill. Serve with other salads and brown bread and butter.

Salmon Trout with Green Herb Sauce

Preparation and cooking time:
2½ hours, plus 2-3 hours cooling time
SERVES 8-10

1 x 4 lb. salmon trout
2 shallots
1 carrot
1 bay leaf
10 fl. oz. [1¼ cups] white wine (optional)
1 pint [2½ cups] water
2 stalks of celery
For the Sauce:
3-4 large spinach leaves
3-4 sprigs of parsley, tarragon and chervil
10 fl. oz. [1¼ cups] mayonnaise (see page 61)
2 tablespoons double [heavy] cream
For the garnish:
5 fl. oz. [⅝ cup] aspic prepared from aspic crystals
cucumber slices
lemon slices
mustard and cress [watercress]

Rinse the fish well under cold running water. Peel and slice the shallots and carrot. Slice the celery.
Put the prepared vegetables in a fish kettle and add the bay leaf, water and wine. Bring to the boil.
Lower the fish into the fish kettle and cover with the lid. Lower the heat and poach very gently for 30-40 minutes.
To test if the fish is cooked, pull the fins gently. If they come away from the body quite easily, the fish is cooked.
If a fish kettle is not available, place the fish in a large meat tin. Add the wine, water and other ingredients, and cover with buttered aluminium foil.
Bake in a moderate oven, 350°F (Gas Mark 4, 180°C), for about 1 hour. Baste the fish frequently and apply the same test as above to see if it is cooked.
When the fish is cooked, remove from the heat and set aside to cool in the cooking liquid.
Meanwhile, to make the sauce cook the spinach and herbs for 5 minutes in a little boiling salted water. Drain well and cool. Chop the spinach and herbs finely and mix with the mayonnaise.

Stir in the cream just before serving.
Prepare the aspic jelly according to the manufacturer's instructions on the packet. Do not let it set.
When the fish is cold, remove it from the cooking liquid and drain. Carefully peel off the skin, starting at the tail but do not remove the tail or the head.
Place the fish on a large serving dish and brush with liquid aspic several times.
Decorate with cucumber and lemon slices and brush again with aspic. The jelly will set and is applied to prevent the fish and decoration from drying out.
Garnish with mustard and cress, and serve with the sauce.

Note: making aspic jelly is a long process and commercial aspic jelly crystals or mixes are quite satisfactory to use.

Goujons de Sole Provençale

Strips of sole Provence-style

Preparation and cooking time:
45-60 minutes
SERVES 4

1 large onion
2 cloves of garlic
4 tomatoes
2 small green peppers
2 oz. [4 tablespoons] butter
8 fl. oz. [1 cup] fish stock or fish stock and white wine
1 tablespoon chopped parsley
¼ teaspoon salt
⅛ teaspoon freshly milled black pepper
8 black olives, halved and stoned
4 fillets of sole
vegetable oil for deep frying
1 egg, beaten
breadcrumbs for coating
To garnish:
Parsley sprigs

Peel and chop the onion, garlic and tomatoes. Core and chop the green pepper.
Melt the butter and sauté the onion, garlic and green pepper for 5 minutes. Add the tomatoes and cook for a further 5 minutes.
Add the stock, or stock and wine, parsley and seasoning and simmer for 15-20 minutes.
Meanwhile, cut the sole fillets into 1-inch wide strips. Coat with egg and

breadcrumbs. Heat the oil until
it is sufficiently hot. Then, deep
fry the sole strips in batches for 3-4
minutes. Drain each batch well on
absorbent kitchen paper.
When the sauce is almost cooked, add
the black olives for the last 2-3
minutes.
Place the goujons of sole in a shallow
serving dish, garnished with parsley.
Serve the sauce in a separate dish.

Prawn Pilaff

Preparation and cooking time:
30 minutes
SERVES 2-3

1 large onion
3 stalks of celery
2 oz. [4 tablespoons] butter
8 oz. [1⅓ cups] long-grain rice
½ teaspoon ground coriander
¼ teaspoon saffron powder
1 pint [2½ cups] chicken stock
6 fl. oz. double [¾ cup heavy] cream
12 oz. prawns or shrimps, shelled
½ teaspoon freshly milled black
     pepper

Peel and chop the onion. Slice the
celery thinly.
Heat the butter and sauté the onions
and celery for 3 minutes.
Add the rice and sauté until it
becomes opaque.
Add the coriander and saffron powder
and stir in the stock. Cover tightly
and simmer for 12-15 minutes or until
all the liquid has been absorbed and
the rice is tender.
Heat together the cream, prawns or
shrimps and freshly milled black
pepper for 3 minutes.
Arrange the rice in a ring on 2 or 3
individual serving dishes and spoon
the prawns or shrimps and cream
mixture into the centre of each ring.
Serve immediately.

Red Mullet
with Fennel

Preparation and cooking time:
1 hour
SERVES 4

4 small red mullets
1 large onion, peeled and thinly
     sliced

1 small bulb of fennel, trimmed
     and finely chopped
2 oz. [4 tablespoons] melted butter
To garnish:
8 lemon wedges
1 tablespoon chopped parsley

Heat the oven to 350°F (Gas Mark 4,
180°C).
Gut the mullet and rinse well. Make
three small incisions across one side of
each fish.
Heat half of the butter and sauté the
onion until soft. Add the fennel and
transfer to an ovenproof casserole.
Place the red mullet on top of the
fennel and brush with the remaining
melted butter. Cover with a lid or
aluminium foil for the first 30 minutes
of cooking only.
Bake on the top shelf of the preheated
oven for 30 minutes and remove the
lid. Continue cooking for 10-15
minutes or until the flesh is firm.
Brush the fish with a little more
melted butter during cooking, if
necessary.
Garnish with chopped parsley and
serve with lemon wedges.

Bouchées aux
Fruits de Mer
Small pastry cases with shellfish
filling

Preparation and cooking time:
40 minutes
SERVES 4

1 lb. puff pastry (see page 61)
beaten egg for glazing
10 fl. oz. [1¼ cups] Béchamel sauce
     (see page 61)
2 hard-boiled eggs
8 oz. fresh or canned white crabmeat
     cartilage removed
4 oz. prawns or shrimps, shelled
1 teaspoon anchovy essence, or
     1 teaspoon anchovy paste mixed
     with 2 drops vinegar

Heat the oven to 425°F (Gas Mark 7,
220°C).
Roll the pastry to ¼-½ inch thickness.
Using a 2½-inch plain pastry cutter,
cut out about 12 rounds and place on
a wet baking tray. Using 1½-inch
plain pastry cutter, make a circle in
the middle of each round, cutting
about a quarter-way through the
pastry. Set aside in a cold place for 20
minutes.
Brush the bouchée cases with beaten

egg and bake on the top shelf of the
preheated oven for about 25 minutes.
Cool slightly.
Using a sharp knife, cut out the small
inner circle from each round and keep
to one side. Scoop out the soft mixture
inside. Keep the bouchée cases hot.
Shell and chop the eggs, and mix them
in a small saucepan with the Béchamel
sauce, crabmeat, prawns or shrimps
and anchovy essence. Heat through
gently over low heat.
Fill the warm bouchée cases with the
the seafood filling, replace the lids and
garnish with a small sprig of parsley.
Serve hot.

Lobster
Thermidor

Cooking and preparation time:
1 hour
SERVES 2

1 x 1½ lbs. cooked lobster
5 fl. oz. [⅝ cup] Béchamel sauce
     (see note below)
2 tablespoons double [heavy] cream
2 tablespoons dry sherry
½ teaspoon chopped tarragon
½ teaspoon chopped chervil
½ teaspoon mustard
1 teaspoon butter
1 tablespoon grated Parmesan
     cheese

Heat the grill [broiler] at its highest
setting.
Split the lobster in half lengthwise,
taking care not to damage the shells.
Take out the flesh and chop it
coarsely. Crack the claws, remove the
flesh and cut it into small pieces.
Reserve the shells.
Mix the Béchamel sauce in a medium-
sized saucepan with the cream,
sherry, tarragon, chervil and mustard.
Add the lobster flesh and warm
through over low heat but do not boil.
Spoon the mixture into the lobster
shells, sprinkle with Parmesan cheese
and dot with butter.
Grill [broil] until lightly browned.
Serve immediately.

Note: Follow the recipe given on
page 61, but double the amount of
flour and butter to make the sauce
very thick.

opposite: Marinated Herrings

LIGHT MEALS

Often in hot weather a single light dish is all that's wanted for a meal. And whether this is at lunchtime or in the evening, these recipes answer the problem in tasty ways. You might like to add a crisp salad, or some crunchy bread with butter—but all are delicious served on their own as well.

Eggs make an ideal basis for a light dish—as with the Oeufs Florentine, the Eggs in Cress Baskets and the Cheese Pancakes. And fish—low in carbohydrate, high in protein—as well as kidneys and vegetables provide excellent nourishment without heaviness.

Two recipes for dishes to accompany any light meal of salad, omelette or cold meat.
left: Eggs in Cress Baskets
below: Danish Ham Salad

Danish Ham Salad

Preparation time:
15 minutes
SERVES 4-6

8 oz. cooked ham, in one piece
8 oz. brisket of beef [corned beef],
  in one piece
1 large or 2 medium-sized pickled
  beetroots [beets]
2 large potatoes, cooked
2 large carrots
1 large onion
1 red eating apple
6 tablespoons beetroot [beet] juice
French dressing (see page 38)

Cut the ham and brisket [corned beef]
into ½ inch squares. Dice the beetroots
[beets] and potatoes to a similar size.
Peel and dice the carrots and onions.
Core and dice the apple.
Toss all the prepared ingredients
together in a large bowl. Add the
beetroot [beet] juice and French
dressing and toss again.
Serve with other salads.

Cheese Pancakes

Preparation and cooking time:
1 hour
SERVES 4

10 fl. oz. [1¼ cup] pancake batter
  (see page 61)
vegetable oil
10 fl. oz. [1¼ cups] Béchamel sauce
  (see page 61)
8 oz. canned tuna fish or salmon
8 tablespoons grated cheese
grated zest of 1 lemon
⅛ teaspoon freshly milled black
  pepper
salt
To garnish:
chopped chives

Prepare the pancake batter.
Heat a small amount of oil in a frying
pan. Pour out and reserve any excess
oil, leaving the pan lightly greased.
Pour a little batter into the pan,
tilting the pan in all directions until
the batter spreads all over the base
of the pan. Cook the pancake until

lightly browned underneath; turn over
and lightly brown the other side.
Turn the pancake on to a warm plate
and keep it hot. Continue in this way
until all the batter has been used,
making 8-12 pancakes.
Divide the Béchamel sauce in half.
Into one half mix the tuna fish or
salmon, the lemon zest, pepper and
salt; and heat it through slowly. Into
the other half, mix the grated cheese;
heat slowly until the cheese melts.
Put a little of the fish mixture in the
centre of each pancake. Roll up and
place 2-3 pancakes on each individual
serving dish. Pour a little of the cheese
sauce over the pancakes and sprinkle
with chopped chives.
Serve immediately.

Variation:
Fill the pancakes with sliced
bananas sprinkled with lemon juice
and sugar and serve with a sweet sauce
and grated chocolate.

Devilled Madeira Kidneys

Preparation and cooking time:
30 minutes
SERVES 4

1¼ lb. lamb's kidneys
1 large onion
1 oz. [2 tablespoons] butter
1½ tablespoons flour
2 teaspoons mild curry powder
½ teaspoon salt
¼ teaspoon freshly milled black
  pepper
1 tablespoon wine vinegar
2 tablespoons dry Madeira or white
  wine (optional)
5 fl. oz. [⅝ cup] beef stock
To garnish:
chopped parsley

Remove and discard any skin and fat
on the kidneys and slice them thinly.
Peel and chop the onion and sauté in
the butter until soft but not browned.
Mix together the flour, curry powder,
salt and pepper and sprinkle over the
the kidneys.
When the onion is soft, add the
kidneys and sauté for about 5
minutes.
Stir in the vinegar, Madeira and stock.
Simmer the kidneys for 15-20 minutes
until the sauce has thickened and the
kidneys are tender.

Serve with sauté potatoes and
Haricots Verts Mignonette (see
page 33).

Baked Crab Savoury

Preparation and cooking time:
30 minutes
SERVES 4

8 oz. canned or frozen crabmeat,
  cartilage removed
2 eggs
4 tablespoons mayonnaise
grated zest of 1 lemon
¼ teaspoon freshly milled black
  pepper
12 canned anchovy fillets
4 slices bread and butter

Heat the oven to 375°F (Gas Mark 5,
190°C).
Mix the crab meat with the egg yolks,
mayonnaise, lemon zest and pepper.
Whisk the egg whites until stiff and
fold into the crab mixture.
Place 3 anchovy fillets on each slice
of bread, then spoon the crab mixture
on top.
Bake on the middle shelf of the preheated oven for 10 minutes.
Serve hot with a mixed salad.

Eggs in Cress Baskets

Preparation and cooking time:
20 minutes
SERVES 2-3

4 eggs
1 tablespoon butter
½ teaspoon anchovy essence, or
  ½ teaspoon anchovy paste mixed
  with 2 drops of vinegar.
2 teaspoons lemon juice
¼ teaspoon Madras curry powder
pinch dry mustard
watercress

Hard boil the eggs, shell them and
cut them in half lengthwise.
Remove the yolks from the whites.
Blend the yolks with the butter,
anchovy essence, lemon juice, curry
powder and mustard. Beat well until

the mixture is soft enough to pipe.
Using a forcing bag and large star
nozzle, pipe the egg mixture into the
egg white halves.
Arrange on a bed of watercress and
serve with a tomato salad and crisp
French bread.

Variations:
§ Mix the egg yolks with 3 tablespoons
cream cheese or 2 tablespoons grated
Cheddar cheese and a little milk to
soften.
§ Mix the egg yolk with 2 oz. liver
pâté and a little butter to soften.
§ Mix the egg yolks with 2 tablespoons
finely chopped ham, 1 teaspoon grated
horseradish and mayonnaise to soften.

Smoked Haddock Ring

Preparation and cooking time:
40 minutes
S E R V E S 4

6 oz. [1 cup] **long-grain rice**
1½ lb. **smoked haddock**
5 fl. oz. [⅝ cup] **milk**
5 fl. oz. [⅝ cup] **water**
1 **shallot**
1 oz. [2 tablespoons] **butter**
2 **hard-boiled eggs, peeled and
    chopped**
1 tablespoon **chopped parsley**
3-4 tablespoons **single [light] cream
    or top of the milk**
¼ teaspoon **freshly milled black
    pepper**
To garnish:
1 **hard-boiled egg, thinly sliced**
pinch of paprika

Cook the rice in boiling salted water
for 15 minutes or until tender and
drain well.
Poach the haddock in the milk and
water for about 15 minutes. Drain and
cool. Remove and discard any skin
and bones from the fish. Flake the
haddock and mix with the rice.
Sauté the shallot in the butter until
soft but not browned. Add the
haddock and rice, chopped egg,
parsley, cream and freshly milled
black pepper. Heat through thoroughly
over low heat, stirring frequently.
Pour the mixture into a ring mould
and press firmly with the back of a
spoon. Turn out on to a hot plate.
Garnish with slices of hard-boiled egg

and a pinch of paprika.
Serve with a green salad.

Oeufs Florentine

Eggs on spinach

Preparation and cooking time:
30 minutes
S E R V E S 4

8 oz. **frozen chopped spinach,
    thawed**
2 oz. [4 tablespoons] **butter**
white pepper
salt
4 **eggs**
10 fl. oz. [1¼ cups] **Béchamel sauce**
    (see page 61)
4 oz. [1 cup] **grated cheese**
1 teaspoon **paprika**

Heat the oven to 400°F (Gas Mark 6,
200°C).
Gently heat the spinach with the butter
until hot and well-blended. Season
with the pepper and salt. Divide the
spinach into 4 individual dishes.
Poach the eggs very lightly and place
an egg in each dish on the spinach.
Mix half of the cheese with the
Béchamel sauce and pour it over the
eggs. Sprinkle them with the
remaining grated cheese and the
paprika.
Bake on the top shelf of the preheated
oven for 10 minutes until golden
brown.
Serve immediately.

Potato and Onion Bake

Preparation and cooking time:
1½ hours
S E R V E S 4

2-3 lbs. **potatoes**
1 lb. **onions**
salt
freshly milled black pepper
1 oz. [2 tablespoons] **butter**
8 oz. **thinly sliced streaky bacon,
    rind removed**
4 **tomatoes, sliced**
6 oz. **Cheddar cheese, thinly sliced**

Heat the oven to 400°F (Gas Mark 6,
200°C).
Peel and thinly slice the potatoes and
onions and place in layers in a deep
ovenproof casserole. Season each layer
with pepper and salt and dot with the
butter. Cover with a lid or aluminium
foil and bake in the preheated oven.
After 1 hour, uncover the casserole
and arrange the bacon slices on top.
Return to the top shelf of the oven
and cook uncovered for a further
10-15 minutes or until the bacon
becomes crisp.
Cover the bacon with the slices of
cheese and tomato and cook without
the lid for 5 minutes or until the
cheese just melts.
Serve hot.

Cauliflower and Mushroom Grill

Preparation and cooking time:
25 minutes
S E R V E S 4

1 large **cauliflower**
4 oz. **mushrooms**
4 oz. **streaky bacon, chopped**
6 oz. [1½ cups] **grated cheese**
5 fl. oz. **double [⅝ cup heavy] cream**
To garnish:
watercress

Trim the cauliflower and cut into
quarters. Cook in boiling salted
water for 10 minutes or until just
tender. Drain well and keep hot in a
flameproof serving dish.
Meanwhile, rinse and chop the
mushrooms.
Grill [broil] the bacon pieces until
partly cooked, then add the
mushrooms and continue cooking for
3-4 minutes, turning the mixture
frequently. Remove with a draining
spoon and place in the dish with the
cauliflower.
Completely cover the cauliflower with
the grated cheese and pour the cream
over the top. Grill [broil] for 3-4
minutes until the cheese melts and
turns golden brown.
Garnish with watercress and serve
immediately with grilled [broiled]
tomatoes and crisp French bread and
butter.

*opposite: Sweet Pancakes
see variation for Cheese Pancakes*

MAIN COURSE MEAT DISHES

A range of meat dishes with lots of variety to satisfy everyone. Lamb and veal are often at their best during the summer months—and here we have chosen five recipes which use these meats with imagination and interest. Each combines flavours-with-a-difference: lamb with the tartness of lemon; the richness of garlic and rosemary; the tang of fresh apricots: veal escalopes in a spicy sauce, and the classic Italian summer favourite, Vitello Tonnato (cold veal in a tuna fish sauce). And as an extra bonus, notes on the preparation of meats for cold platters.

left: Piquant Calf's Liver
below: Steak Flambé

Lamb with Lemon

☆ ☆　　① ①　　◫ ◫

Preparation and cooking time:
30 minutes, plus 2-3 hours marinating time
S E R V E S　4

8 lamb chops
1 shallot or small onion
8 lemon slices
3 tablespoons lemon juice
2 tablespoons vegetable oil
1 bay leaf
½ teaspoon mixed herbs
½ teaspoon salt
¼ teaspoon lemon pepper
1 tablespoon flour
1-2 eggs, beaten
4 oz. [2 cups] fresh breadcrumbs
3 oz. [⅜ cup] butter

Trim any excess fat from the chops. Peel and finely chop the shallot. Place the meat in a large bowl with the onion, lemon slices, lemon juice, oil, herbs and seasoning. Mix well together and set aside to marinate for 2-3 hours. Turn the chops frequently in the marinade.
Drain the meat and dust lightly with the flour. Brush with beaten egg and coat with the breadcrumbs.
Melt the butter in a frying pan and fry the chops on one side for 5-7 minutes. Turn them over and place a lemon slice from the marinade on each one. Cook for a further 5-7 minutes. Press the lemon slices occasionally to squeeze out any remaining juice.
Serve the chops with new potatoes and Beetroot with Orange. (See page 33).

Agneau a là Boulangère

Roast lamb

☆　　　① ①　　◫ ◫

Preparation and cooking time:
1½-2 hours
S E R V E S　6-8

1 x 4 lb. leg of lamb
2 cloves of garlic, quartered
　　lengthwise
12 small sprigs of fresh or
　　1 tablespoon dried rosemary
3 oz. [⅜ cup] butter
1 teaspoon salt
3 lb. potatoes

2 large onions
freshly milled black pepper
3 tablespoons stock or water
To garnish:
chopped parsley

Heat the oven to 400°F (Gas Mark 6, 200°C).
Using a sharp pointed knife, make 6-8 small slits in the leg of lamb. Press one quarter clove of garlic and a small sprig of rosemary into each slit. If using dried rosemary, roll the garlic in it before inserting the garlic. Spread the lamb with the butter and sprinkle with salt.
Peel and slice the potatoes and onions very thinly and place these in layers in a large roasting pan. Sprinkle each layer with salt and pepper, adding a sprig of fresh, or ½ teaspoon dried, rosemary. Pour the stock or water over the potato mixture and place the leg of lamb on the top. If you want the meat to be pink and slightly underdone, keep the oven at 400°F and roast the meat for 1-1¼ hours. If you prefer well-done lamb, reduce the heat after 1 hour to 350°F (Gas Mark 4, 180°C) and roast the meat for a further 30-40 minutes.
Transfer the lamb to a serving plate for carving. Place the potatoes in a hot serving dish and sprinkle with chopped parsley.
Serve with Haricots Verts Mignonette (See page 33) and a thin gravy.

Pork Olives

☆ ☆　　① ①　　◫ ◫

Preparation and cooking time:
1¼ hours
S E R V E S　4

2 x 12 oz. pork fillets
8 prunes, soaked in water overnight
1 cooking apple
¼ teaspoon salt
¼ teaspoon freshly milled black
　　pepper
¼ teaspoon powdered rosemary
2 oz. [4 tablespoons] butter
4 tablespoons tomato purée
10 fl. oz. [1¼ cups] water
1 bay leaf
5 fl. oz. single [⅝ cup light] cream

Using a sharp knife, slit each fillet halfway through from one end to the other. Open out the fillets and pound with a rolling pin until slightly flattened. Halve and stone the prunes. Peel, core and thinly slice the apple.

Arrange the prune and apple pieces in the centre of each fillet. Sprinkle with salt, pepper and rosemary. Using a large needle and strong thread sew the edges together to enclose the fruit completely.
Melt the butter in a frying pan and fry each fillet quickly until lightly browned.
Add the tomato purée, water and bay leaf, then cover and simmer for 25-30 minutes.
Add the cream and cook gently for a further 10 minutes until the pork is tender.
Serve with sauté potatoes and sweet-corn.

Roast Fillet of Beef with Béarnaise Sauce

☆ ☆ ☆　① ① ①　◫ ◫

Preparation and cooking time:
1 hour 20 minutes
S E R V E S　8-10

1 x 4 lb. fillet of beef (see note
　　below)
2 tablespoons olive oil
For the sauce:
2 shallots
2 sprigs fresh, or 1 teaspoon each
　　dried, tarragon and chervil
6 tablespoons tarragon vinegar
4 tablespoons white wine
6 peppercorns
1 bay leaf
8 oz. [1 cup] softened butter
2 teaspoons mixed chopped tarragon
　　and chervil (fresh if possible)

Heat the oven to 400°F (Gas Mark 6, 200°C).
Brush the beef all over with the olive oil and place it on a rack in a roasting pan. Place in the oven and cook for 50 minutes for the meat to be rare or 1 hour 15 minutes for it to be quite well done. Baste frequently with the pan juices.
To make the sauce, peel and finely chop the shallot and place it in a saucepan with the sprigs of tarragon and chervil, vinegar, wine, peppercorns and bay leaf. Boil until reduced to about 1 tablespoon. Strain.
Place the egg yolks in a bowl over a saucepan of hot water. Add the strained liquid and 1 tablespoon of the butter. Mix well with a small wooden spoon or with a small wire whisk.

Continue to add the butter, a little at a time, stirring continuously. As the mixture thickens, continue to stir until all the butter has been added. Remove from the heat and stir in the chopped chervil and tarragon.
Keep the sauce warm but do not allow it to boil because it may curdle.
Serve the beef and sauce accompanied by green beans and new potatoes.

Note: A smaller piece of the fillet may be cooked in the same way.

Veal with Paprika Sauce

Preparation and cooking time:
50 minutes
SERVES 4

4 x 5 oz. veal escalopes
2 tablespoons sweet paprika
1 medium-sized onion, peeled and chopped
2 cloves of garlic, peeled and chopped
1 lb. tomatoes, peeled and chopped
2 oz. mushrooms, chopped
3 oz. [⅜ cup] butter
2 teaspoons caraway seeds
10 fl. oz. [1¼ cups] veal or chicken stock
½ teaspoon salt
¼ teaspoon freshly milled black pepper
2 tablespoons sweet sherry
2 tablespoons double [heavy] cream

Lightly pound the escalopes with a rolling pin until very thin. Sprinkle liberally with the paprika.
Melt half of the butter in a frying pan and sauté the escalopes for 3-4 minutes on each side. Remove from the pan and keep warm. Melt the remaining butter in the same pan and sauté the onion and garlic until soft but not browned. Add the tomatoes, mushrooms and caraway seeds and sauté for about 10 minutes.
Add the stock, salt and pepper and simmer for about 15 minutes or until the tomatoes are very soft.
Press the mixture through a strainer to reduce to a purée.
Return the veal escalopes to the pan, and add the purée, the sherry and cream and simmer for about 5 minutes until the veal is thoroughly heated. Adjust the seasoning of the sauce, adding more cream, if required.

Serve with crisp sauté potatoes and green peas.

Quick-fried Chinese Steak

Preparation and cooking time:
15 minutes
SERVES 2

1 leek
1 green pepper
1 red pepper
2 oz. mushrooms
2 tablespoons sesame oil (see page 26)
4 oz. fresh or canned bean sprouts
3 tablespoons soy sauce
2 x 4-6 oz. fillet steaks

Trim the leek and separate the layers. Rinse thoroughly under cold running water and dry well. Shred finely.
Core and chop the peppers. Slice the mushrooms thinly.
Heat half of the oil in a frying pan and sauté the chopped peppers for 5 minutes. Add the leek and mushroom slices and sauté for 3-4 minutes.
Stir in the bean sprouts and soy sauce and heat for 1 minute.
Transfer to a warmed serving plate and keep hot.
Heat the remaining oil until very hot. Fry the steaks for 2-3 minutes on each side, to taste.
Place the steaks on top of the vegetables and serve immediately with boiled or fried rice and Chinese cabbage.

Piquant Calf's Liver

Preparation and cooking time:
20 minutes
SERVES 4

4 oz. [½ cup] butter
1½ lb. calf's or lamb's liver
5 tablespoons lemon juice
2 tablespoons finely chopped shallot or onion
1 tablespoon chopped parsley

Melt half of the butter in a frying pan and sauté the slices of liver for 1

minute on each side.
Lower the heat and fry the liver for a further 5 minutes, turning the slices once. Reserve the pan juices.
Meanwhile, melt the remaining butter with the lemon juice. Add the onion and parsley and heat until blended. Add the reserved pan juices.
Serve the liver and sauce with Deep-fried Cauliflower (see page 34) and creamed potatoes.

Lamb and Apricot Kebabs

Preparation and cooking time:
40 minutes, plus overnight marinating time
SERVES 4

2 lb. lean lamb cut into 1-inch cubes
1 lb. fresh apricots, halved and stoned
1 bay leaf, crushed
1 teaspoon salt
1 teaspoon freshly milled black pepper
3 tablespoons sesame oil (see note below)
3 tablespoons lime or lemon juice
1 medium-sized onion, peeled and grated
2 cloves of garlic, peeled and crushed
2 x 1-inch slices sesame seed bread (see note below)

Place the lamb and apricots in a large bowl. Add the bay leaf, salt, pepper, oil, lime or lemon juice, onion and garlic. Mix well together then set aside to marinate for several hours or overnight. Turn the ingredients occasionally in the marinade.
Cut the bread into 1-inch cubes and sprinkle with a little of the marinade. Heat the grill [broiler] at its highest setting.
Thread the cubes of meat, the bread and the apricots alternately on to either 4 long or 8 short metal skewers.
The bread will become quite burnt and charred which adds to the flavour of the kebabs, but if preferred it may be omitted.
Grill [broil] the kebabs for 5 minutes, turning them frequently. Lower the heat and cook for a further 5 minutes or until the meat is well-browned.

opposite: Quick-fried Chinese Steak

Brush with a little of the marinade during cooking.

Serve the kebabs on a bed of rice, accompanied by aubergines [eggplants], thinly sliced and fried in butter, and a tomato salad with French Dressing.

Note: Sesame oil gives a delicious nutty and unusual flavour, but if it is not available, olive oil may be used instead.

Sesame seed bread is available in Greek grocery shops and most delicatessens. It may be replaced by crusty white bread.

Porc Dijon

Pork with Dijon Mustard

Preparation and cooking time:
35 minutes
S E R V E S 4

4 loin pork chops
4 oz. Emmental [Swiss] **or Gruyère cheese**
4 teaspoons Dijon mustard
2 tablespoons double [heavy] **cream**
$\frac{1}{4}$ teaspoon freshly milled black pepper

Heat the grill [broiler] at its highest setting, then turn down the heat slightly, and grill [broil] the chops for about 15-20 minutes, turning them frequently.

Meanwhile, grate the cheese and mix with the mustard, cream and pepper.

Spread the chops with the mixture and grill [broil] for a further 3-4 minutes or until the cheese is golden brown.

Serve immediately with new potatoes and a green salad.

Vitello Tonnato

Cold sliced veal with tuna fish sauce

Preparation and cooking time:
3 hours, plus 3-4 hours cooling time
S E R V E S 6-8

6 anchovy fillets
2 fl. oz. [$\frac{1}{4}$ cup] **milk**
1 x 2 lb. breast of veal, boned and rolled
1 large onion

1 carrot
grated zest and juice of 1 lemon
1 bay leaf
5 fl. oz. [$\frac{5}{8}$ cup] **white wine**
5 fl. oz. [$\frac{5}{8}$ cup] **water**
7-8 oz. canned tuna fish
10 fl. oz. [$1\frac{1}{4}$ cups] **mayonnaise** (see page 61)
2 tablespoons lemon juice
To garnish:
lemon slices

Soak the anchovies in the milk for 10-15 minutes to remove excessive saltiness. Drain the anchovies and halve them. Using a sharp pointed knife, make 12 small slits in the veal and press half an anchovy fillet into each slit.

Peel and slice the onion and carrot and place in a large pan with the veal, lemon zest and juice, bay leaf, white wine and water. Cover and bring to the boil over high heat. Reduce the heat and simmer for 2 hours or until tender.

When the meat is cooked, leave it in the cooking liquid and set aside until cold. Reserve 3 tablespoons of the stock.

To make the sauce, pound the tuna fish to a smooth paste and press through a sieve. Add the mayonnaise, lemon juice and the reserved stock and mix well.

Slice the meat and arrange on a plate. Garnish with slices of lemon and serve with the tuna fish sauce and a variety of salads.

Steak Flambé

Preparation and cooking time:
40 minutes
S E R V E S 2-3

2 oz. [4 tablespoons] **butter**
1 large onion, peeled and chopped
2 cloves of garlic, peeled and chopped
1 green pepper, cored and chopped
4 oz. button mushrooms, sliced
$\frac{1}{2}$ small bulb fennel, thinly sliced
salt and pepper
1 lb. fillet or sirloin steak, cut into 1-inch cubes
3 tomatoes, sliced

Heat half of the butter in a frying pan and sauté the onion, garlic and pepper until almost soft but not browned. Add the mushrooms and fennel and sauté for 5 minutes. Season

with salt and pepper. Remove from the pan and keep hot.

Melt the remaining butter over a very high heat and sauté the cubes of steak until browned all over. Warm the brandy, pour into the pan and set it alight with a taper. Let it burn for 30 seconds then extinguish the flames with a lid and add the hot vegetables and the tomatoes.

Heat through and serve immediately with saffron rice.

Serving Cold Meat

Roast Meat which is cut and served cold will go twice as far as meat sliced when it is hot and, of course, it is always nice to be able to serve cold meat leftovers. Summertime is an ideal time to economize in this way.

Meat cuts should be boned and tied into a compact shape which is easy to carve. Stuffed joints are even tastier when they are served cold.

The addition of flavourings before the meat is cooked is an ideal way of making cold meats a little unusual. Agneau â la Boulangère (page 23) is a good example, providing the leg is boned. As soon as the meat is cooked, take it out of the pan to cool, and do not leave it to cool in a pool of fat.

Always cover the meat and leave it in a cold place for several hours or overnight if possible. Chilled meat cuts very easily.

Boiling is an ideal method of cooking meats to be served cold (see Vitello Tonnato, this page). The meat will be moist and succulent and even the oldest boiling chicken can be made tasty and tender if simmered in a well-flavoured stock.

Again, it is best to bone the meats and although boning a chicken is a little difficult, the effort is well worth it when it comes to serving. A good butcher will bone a chicken for you at little extra charge.

Providing all joints of meat are cooled thoroughly it is possible to keep a joint for 2 or 3 days in a refrigerator. Let the meat cool as quickly as possible, and then wrap in foil or film before storing it.

opposite: Roast Fillet of Beef with Béarnaise Sauce

MAIN COURSE POULTRY DISHES

left: Chicken Risotto
below: Tarragon Chicken

Until recently an expensive luxury in many countries, chicken is now a relatively inexpensive and good buy—especially in the summer when cold leftovers may so readily be turned into tasty salads. Its delicate flavour is especially well-enhanced by the addition of fresh herbs such as tarragon (try the Tarragon Chicken), but also responds well to stronger influences such as garlic and coriander (both are used in Khan Chicken).

Duck is a less common buy, but today quite readily obtained. We've devised a super recipe with a classic orange sauce, as well as the Salmi. And our serving accompaniments make meal-planning easier.

Chicken in Wine Vinegar

Preparation and cooking time:
45 minutes
S E R V E S 4

1 clove of garlic
3 oz. [⅜ cup] unsalted butter
4 chicken joints
6 tablespoons white wine vinegar
4 tablespoons tomato purée
6 teaspoons French mustard
1 teaspoon Worcestershire sauce
¼ teaspoon salt
¼ teaspoon freshly milled black pepper
2 tablespoons white wine or water
4-6 tablespoons double [heavy] cream

Peel the garlic and put in a large casserole or saucepan with the butter. Heat the butter until very hot and when the frothing subsides, add the chicken pieces and fry very quickly until well-browned. Reduce the heat and fry the chicken gently for a further 10 minutes.

Add the wine vinegar, cover and simmer for 10 minutes. Remove the chicken from the pan and keep hot in a serving dish. Discard the garlic.

Blend the tomato purée with the mustard, Worcestershire sauce, salt, pepper and white wine. Stir this mixture into the juices remaining in the pan, making sure to scrape all the sediment from the sides and bottom of the pan. Reduce the liquid by about a quarter.

Remove the pan from the heat and stir in the cream. Pour the sauce over the chicken and serve hot, accompanied by sauté potatoes and courgettes [zucchini].

Chicken Risotto

Preparation and cooking time:
40 minutes
S E R V E S 3-4

1 x 3 lb. chicken, ready-roasted
8 oz. [1⅓ cups] long-grain rice
16 fl. oz. [2 cups] chicken stock
1 large onion
2 oz. [4 tablespoons] butter
2 oz. button mushrooms
4 tablespoons canned or frozen peas
4 fl. oz. tarragon vinegar
1 tablespoon canned red pimientos
1 teaspoon finely chopped fresh tarragon

Chop the chicken meat, discarding the bones.

Rinse the rice well under cold running water and place in a large saucepan with the stock.

Bring to the boil, then cover. Lower the heat and simmer until all the liquid has been absorbed and the rice is tender and dry.

Meanwhile, peel and chop the onion. Heat the butter and sauté the onion until almost soft. Add the mushrooms and sauté for a further 5 minutes.

Add the pieces of chicken, the peas and the tarragon vinegar and heat quickly until the liquid evaporates.

Mix the chicken and vegetables with the rice. Slice the red pimientos and add to the rice and chicken with the tarragon.

Mix together lightly and pile into a hot serving dish.

Serve at once.

Chicken Maryland

Preparation and cooking time:
1 hour
S E R V E S 4

For frying the chicken:
1 x 5 lb. chicken
3 tablespoons flour
½ teaspoon salt
¼ teaspoon freshly milled black pepper
1 egg
3 oz. [1½ cups] fresh breadcrumbs finely grated

3 oz. [6 tablespoons] butter
For the corn fritters:
3 tablespoons plain flour
½ teaspoon baking powder
4 tablespoons fresh breadcrumbs, finely grated
¼ teaspoon salt
1 egg
8 oz. canned or frozen sweetcorn
about 4 fl. oz. [½ cup] milk
For the fried bananas:
2 bananas
1 oz. [2 tablespoons] butter
To garnish:
watercress

Joint the chicken into 8 portions.

Mix together the flour and seasonings.

Coat each chicken portion with the seasoned flour and then with the beaten egg and breadcrumbs.

Melt the butter in a frying pan and fry the pieces of chicken quickly until they are lightly browned all over.

Lower the heat and fry for a further 15-20 minutes, or until tender.

Meanwhile make the fritters by sifting the flour into a bowl, and adding the breadcrumbs, salt, egg and sweetcorn. Mix together gradually adding enough milk to make a thick dropping consistency.

Melt the butter in a frying pan and drop spoonfuls of the corn mixture into the hot fat.

Fry until golden brown then turn the fritters over and cook on the other side.

Peel the bananas and cut each one in half lengthwise. Fry the pieces gently in hot butter on either side until they are lightly browned.

Arrange the chicken on a large, hot serving dish and surround with the fritters and bananas.

Garnish with watercress and serve immediately.

Khan Chicken

Preparation and cooking time:
1¼ hours
S E R V E S 4

1 x 5 lb. chicken
3 tablespoons flour
2 teaspoons ground coriander
¼ teaspoon saffron powder
1 teaspoon salt
½ teaspoon freshly milled black pepper
2 oz. [4 tablespoons] unsalted butter
8 fl. oz. [1 cup] medium-sweet white wine
4 tablespoons double [heavy] cream

Joint the chicken into 8 pieces. Mix together the flour, coriander, saffron, salt and pepper. Toss each piece of chicken in the seasoned flour. Reserve any excess flour.
Melt the butter in a heavy-based frying pan over high heat until the foam subsides and the butter begins to brown. Fry the pieces of chicken very quickly until they are well-browned all over. Remove the pan from the heat, let it cool slightly then add the wine. Cover the pan and simmer the chicken for about 30 minutes or until tender.
Remove the pieces of chicken from the pan and keep hot on a serving dish. Blend the reserved seasoned flour with the cream and stir this into the juices remaining in the pan. Heat gently, stirring continuously until the mixture thickens.
Pour the sauce over the chicken and serve with rice and a green salad.

Duck with Caramelled Orange Sauce

☆ ☆ ① ① ① ⊠ ⊠

Preparation and cooking time:
2 hours
SERVES 4

1 x 5-6 lb. duck
6 oz. [1 cup] long-grain rice
1 large onion, peeled and chopped
2 cloves of garlic, peeled and chopped
2 eating apples, cored and chopped
2 oz. [4 tablespoons] butter
10 fl. oz. [1¼ cups] orange juice
10 fl. oz. [1¼ cups] chicken stock
½ teaspoon salt
3 oz. [½ cup] raisins
2 oranges
2½ oz. [5 tablespoons] sugar
5 tablespoons water
2 tablespoons white wine or cider vinegar
2 teaspoons cornflour [cornstarch]

Heat the oven to 425°F (Gas Mark 7, 220°C).
Prick the duck lightly all over with a needle. Rinse the rice well under cold running water and drain.
Heat the butter in a large saucepan and sauté the onion and garlic until soft but not browned. Add the rice and fry until it becomes opaque.
Add the orange juice, half of the chicken stock and the salt. Simmer until all the liquid has been absorbed, and the rice is just cooked. Remove from the heat and add the apples and raisins, mixing well.
Stuff the duck with the rice mixture and put it on a rack in a roasting pan. Place in the preheated oven and roast for 30 minutes. Reduce the heat to 375°F (Gas Mark 5, 190°C) and roast the duck for a further 45 minutes.
Meanwhile, to make the sauce, pare the zest from the oranges and cut it into very thin slivers. Squeeze the oranges and reserve the juice. Heat the sugar and water in a small heavy-based saucepan, over low heat.
When the sugar has dissolved, increase the heat and boil the liquid until it becomes a deep golden brown caramel. Remove from the heat and immediately add the orange juice, the zest, remaining stock and the vinegar. Simmer gently for 15-20 minutes, or until the zest is tender.
Blend the cornflour with a little water and add this to the orange sauce, stirring continuously over moderate heat until the sauce thickens.
Serve the duck accompanied by the caramelled orange sauce, roast potatoes and green peas.

Tarragon Chicken

Roasted in a clay brick

☆ ☆ ① ① ⊠ ⊠

Preparation and cooking time:
2¼ hours
SERVES 4-5

1 x 5 lb. roasting chicken
2 cloves of garlic
3 oz. [⅜ cup] butter
1 tablespoon chopped fresh, or 2 teaspoons dried, tarragon
5 fl. oz. [⅝ cup] chicken stock
5 fl. oz. [⅝ cup] Béchamel sauce (see page 61)

Soak the clay casserole in water for 10 minutes.
Rinse the chicken and dry well.
Peel and chop the garlic and blend with the butter and tarragon. Stuff the chicken with this mixture.
Place the chicken in the clay casserole and cover with the lid. Place on the middle shelf of a cold oven.
Heat the oven to 450°F (Gas Mark 8, 230°C) and cook the chicken for 1½ hours.
Remove the chicken from the oven and drain all the juices from the casserole. Return the chicken to the oven for 30 minutes without the cover so that the dry heat in the casserole browns and crisps the chicken skin.
Make up the cooking juices to the required amount for the stock with water. Stir in the Béchamel sauce and add extra chopped tarragon, to taste.
Serve the chicken accompanied by the sauce, Pommes Dauphinois and Beetroot with Orange (see page 33).

Salmi of Duck

Casseroled duck with mushrooms

☆ ☆ ① ① ① ⊠ ⊠

Preparation and cooking time:
1½ hours
SERVES 2

1 x 3-4 lb. duck
1 pint [2½ cups] water
bouquet garni
salt and pepper
3 shallots
1 clove of garlic
8 fl. oz. [1 cup] good red wine, claret or burgundy
1 tablespoon brandy
4 oz. button mushrooms

Heat the oven to 425°F (Gas Mark 7, 220°C).
Place the duck on a wire rack and stand in a meat pan. Prick lightly with a fork.
Roast the duck in the preheated oven for 45 minutes. Set aside to cool.
Slice the breast of duck, remove the wings and legs and place them in a flameproof casserole until required.
Put the carcass and skin of the duck in a saucepan, with the water and bouquet garni. Simmer for 30 minutes or until the water is reduced to half. Add salt and pepper to taste. Strain.
Peel and chop the shallot and garlic. Sauté in the butter for 2-3 minutes.
Add the wine and stock and simmer until reduced by half.
Strain the liquid over the duck in the casserole, add the brandy and mushrooms and simmer for 15-20 minutes or until the duck is hot and tender.
Serve with new potatoes and green peas.

---

opposite: Duck with Caramelled Orange Sauce

VEGETABLE ACCOMPANIMENTS

Many vegetable dishes make excellent first course choices for a meal—in this section the Stuffed Cabbage Leaves, Spanish Pimientos, Creamed Mushrooms or Haricots Verts Mignonette would all be ideal served in that way. And well-known vegetables are often neglected through over-use—so here we have varied the cooking method and accompaniments from the usual to give you beetroot in a tangy thick orange sauce, and deep-fried cauliflower florets.

left: Spanish Pimientos
below: Danish Potatoes

Danish Potatoes

Preparation and cooking time:
30 minutes
SERVES 4-6

1 lb. new potatoes
4 oz. castor [½ cup fine] sugar
2 oz. [4 tablespoons] butter
To garnish:
chopped parsley

Thoroughly rinse the potatoes and cook in boiling water for 8-10 minutes, or until tender. Drain and cool, then peel the potatoes and rinse under cold running water. Set aside.
Heat the sugar gently in a large heavy-based saucepan until it melts and begins to turn a golden caramel colour. Mix in the butter and heat until this is melted. Add the potatoes and toss gently over a low heat until they are completely coated with the butter mixture.
Sprinkle with a little chopped parsley and serve hot with roasts or fish dishes.

Note: To save time canned potatoes may be used for this recipe.

Beetroot with Orange

Preparation and cooking time:
45 minutes
SERVES 4

1 lb. cooked beetroot [beets]
1 shallot or small onion
2 cloves of garlic
grated zest and juice of 1 orange
8 fl. oz. [1 cup] orange juice
3 tablespoons wine vinegar
2 tablespoons sugar
1 oz. [2 tablespoons] butter
¼ teaspoon salt
freshly milled black pepper

Peel and dice the beetroot [beets] and place them in a saucepan. Peel and chop the shallot and garlic cloves. Add these and the remaining ingredients to the beetroot [beets].
Bring to the boil, lower the heat and simmer for about 30 minutes with the pan covered. Remove the lid and continue simmering until the excess fluid has evaporated and a thick syrup-like sauce remains in the pan.

Serve immediately. If you do find it necessary to keep the dish hot, take care that the sauce does not burn. When re-heating the contents, keep the pan over very low heat and add 2-3 tablespoons of water.

Haricots Verts Mignonnette

French beans with ground nutmeg

Preparation and cooking time:
35 minutes
SERVES 4-6

1 lb. French [green] beans
2 oz. [4 tablespoons] butter
4 tablespoons double [heavy] cream
½ teaspoon freshly milled black pepper
½ teaspoon freshly grated nutmeg

Top and tail the beans and rinse them well. Cook in boiling salted water for 15-20 minutes, or until tender.
Drain thoroughly and leave the beans uncovered in a warm place for 2-3 minutes to make sure all the water evaporates.
Add the butter, cream, pepper and nutmeg, and toss together until all the beans are well-coated.
Serve hot.

Pommes Dauphinois

Sliced potatoes with cream

Preparation and cooking time:
1½ hours
SERVES 4-6

1½ lb. potatoes
1 clove of garlic
3 oz. [⅜ cup] butter
¼-½ teaspoon salt
¼ teaspoon freshly grated nutmeg
4 fl. oz. single [½ cup light] cream, or milk
4 fl. oz. double [½ cup heavy] cream

Heat oven to 400°F (Gas Mark 6, 200°C).
Peel the potatoes and cut them into thin slices. Peel and crush the garlic and blend with a quarter of the butter. Spread the mixture over the inside of

a shallow baking dish. Arrange the potatoes in layers and season each layer with salt. Sprinkle the top with nutmeg and pour the cream over the entire contents. Cut the remaining butter into small pieces and place on the top.
Put the potatoes in the pre-heated oven for 15 minutes, then lower the heat to 350°F (Gas Mark 4, 180°C) and cook for a further 45 minutes to 1 hour.
Serve immediately.

Spanish Pimientos

Preparation and cooking time:
1 hour
SERVES 4

4 green peppers
4 oz. mushrooms
1 large onion
1 clove of garlic
2 tomatoes
2 oz. [4 tablespoons] butter
8 oz. minced [ground] beef
8 oz. [3¼ cups] cooked rice
1 tablespoon chopped fresh dillweed
3 tablespoons tomato purée
½ teaspoon salt
¼ teaspoon freshly milled black pepper
10 fl. oz. [1¼ cups] beef stock

Heat the oven to 400°F (Gas Mark 6, 200°C).
Cut the tops off the peppers and keep these separate. Scoop the pith and seeds out of the peppers, and discard them.
Rinse and dry the peppers and mushrooms. Peel and chop the onion, garlic and tomatoes. Heat the butter and sauté the onion and garlic for 5 minutes.
Add the mushrooms and meat and cook for 10 minutes, stirring frequently.
Stir in the rice, tomatoes, dillweed, tomato purée, salt and pepper and enough of the stock to moisten the mixture.
Spoon the mixture into the peppers and replace the lids. Place the peppers in a casserole and add the remaining stock. Cover with a lid and bake in the middle shelf of the preheated oven for 35-40 minutes or until the peppers are tender.
Serve immediately.

Creamed Mushrooms

 ① ① ☒

Preparation and cooking time:
20 minutes
S E R V E S 4

12 oz. button mushrooms
1 tablespoon lemon juice
1 oz. [2 tablespoons] butter
3 fl. oz. [⅜ cup] medium-sweet white
   wine
2 tablespoons flour
4 fl. oz. double [½ cup heavy] cream
¼-½ teaspoon freshly milled black
   pepper
salt

Rinse the mushrooms then slice them
thickly and place them in a saucepan
with the lemon juice, butter and wine.
Simmer for about 10 minutes or until
the mushrooms are tender.
Blend the flour with the cream and
stir into the mushrooms. Heat gently,
stirring continuously until the mixture
thickens. Do not allow it to boil. Add
the seasoning according to taste.
Serve immediately with fish or roast
meats, or as a first course with crisp
garlic bread.

Stuffed Cabbage Leaves

 ① ☒ ☒

Preparation and cooking time:
1½ hours
S E R V E S 4

1 small firm cabbage
1 onion
4 oz. [½ cup] butter
4 tablespoons long-grain rice
16 fl. oz. [2 cups] beef stock
8 oz. minced [ground] beef
1 tablespoon chopped fresh parsley
½ teaspoon dried sweet basil
1 teaspoon tomato purée
¼ teaspoon salt
¼ teaspoon freshly milled black
   pepper

Heat the oven to 350°F (Gas Mark 4,
180°C).
Trim off and discard any damaged
outer leaves of the cabbage. Place the
cabbage in a pan of boiling water and
cook for 15 minutes. Drain and cool.
Meanwhile, peel and chop the onion,

melt one third of the butter in a frying
pan and sauté the rice until it becomes
opaque. Add the onion and sauté for
3-4 minutes. Add half of the beef
stock and simmer until all the liquid
has been absorbed and the rice is just
cooked.
Mix the rice with the minced [ground]
beef, parsley, basil, tomato purée, salt
and pepper.
Remove the leaves of the cabbage, one
by one, taking care not to break them.
Spread the leaves out and place a little
of the meat mixture on each one. Fold
the edges into the centre then roll up
the leaves to enclose the filling
completely.
Place close together in a buttered
ovenproof dish. Pour over the
remaining stock and dot with the
remaining butter.
Bake for about 1 hour and serve hot.

Mixed Vegetable Curry

 ① ①

Cooking and preparation time:
1½ hours
S E R V E S 4-6

1 lb. new potatoes
1 small cauliflower
4 courgettes [zucchini]
1 large aubergine [eggplant]
8 oz. ladies fingers' [okra]
2 large onions
3 cloves of garlic
3 tablespoons flour
1 teaspoon salt
½ teaspoon freshly milled black
   pepper
2 tablespoons mild curry powder
1 teaspoon turmeric
4 teaspoons ground coriander
3 tablespoons vegetable oil
4 tablespoons tomato purée
1 bay leaf
2 dried chillis
5 fl. oz. [⅝ cup] stock
2 fl. oz. [¼ cup] milk or cream
   (optional)

Scrape the potatoes and rinse under
cold running water. Cut into small
pieces.
Break the cauliflower into small sprigs.
Slice the courgettes [zucchini] thickly
and cut the aubergine [eggplant] into
similar sized pieces.
Using a stainless steel knife, trim the
stalks from the ladies' fingers [okra],
taking care not to cut too low and

expose the seeds inside.
Peel and slice the onions and garlic.
Mix together the flour, salt, pepper,
curry powder, turmeric and coriander.
Toss the potatoes, cauliflower,
courgettes [zucchini] and aubergines
[eggplant] in the seasoned flour.
Shake off and reserve any excess flour.
Heat the oil in a large saucepan and
sauté the onions and garlic for 5
minutes.
Remove from the pan and reserve.
Sauté the tossed vegetables in the pan,
adding them a few at a time to prevent
them from sticking to the sides of the
pan.
Add the onions and garlic, any excess
flour, the bay leaf, chillies and stock
mixed with the tomato purée.
Cover tightly and simmer for about
30 minutes or until the vegetables are
cooked but still firm.
During cooking, the vegetables will
produce their own liquid, but add a
little more stock if necessary.
Alternatively, stir in milk or cream
just before serving.
Serve with boiled rice and chutney.

Deep~fried Cauliflower

 ①

Preparation and cooking time:
35 minutes
S E R V E S 4

1 large cauliflower
3-4 tablespoons French Dressing
   (see page 38)
1 large egg, beaten
4 oz. [2 cups] fresh breadcrumbs
vegetable oil for deep frying
8 tablespoons finely-grated cheese

Break the cauliflower into fairly large
sprigs and cook in boiling salted water
until it begins to soften. Drain well and
place on a large plate. Sprinkle with
the French Dressing and set aside
until cold.
Heat the oil for deep frying.
Coat each sprig of cauliflower with
egg and breadcrumbs and deep fry
them in the hot oil until they are
crisp and golden brown. Drain well
and place in a hot serving dish.
Sprinkle with cheese and serve
immediately.

opposite: Stuffed Cabbage Leaves

SALADS & SALAD DRESSINGS

left: Cucumber Salad
below: Seafood Salad

Salads are a natural choice for the summer—but this doesn't mean that they are always well-prepared or appetizing. Limp lettuce leaves smothered in cheap dressing, canned beetroot [beets], tired watery tomatoes—too often these masquerade as the real thing. Yet only a few simple rules need be observed to create a delightful dish. The ingredients (especially the lettuce if this is used) must be really fresh; if washed it must also be thoroughly dried. The dressing should be a light one (not more than one part of vinegar to 3 of oil, for example). And once dressed, a salad must be served at once.

Spicy Beetroot Salad

 ① ☒ ☒ ☒

Preparation time:
10 minutes, plus overnight cooling time
SERVES 4

1 lb. cooked beetroot [beets]
4 dill-pickled cucumbers, thinly sliced
2 tablespoons freshly grated horseradish
few drops of Tabasco sauce
6 teaspoons castor [fine] sugar
4 tablespoons tarragon vinegar

Peel and dice the beetroot [beets] and place in a bowl. Add the dill pickles to the beetroot [beets], together with the horseradish and the Tabasco sauce.
Heat the sugar and vinegar together until the sugar has dissolved. Pour this over the beetroot [beets].
Set aside in a cold place for several hours or overnight.

Seafood Salad

 ① ① ① ☒

Preparation time:
15 minutes
SERVES 3-4

12 oz. cooked white fish, such as cod, haddock or hake
8 oz. prawns or shrimps, shelled
lettuce leaves, washed
chopped chives

Remove and discard the skin and bones from the fish, and flake the flesh with a fork.
Line a salad bowl with lettuce leaves, or arrange them on a plate, and pile the flaked fish and most of the prawns into the centre.
Garnish with reserved prawns and chopped chives.
Serve with the Prawn Cocktail Mayonnaise (see page 62).

Variations:
Any seafoods may be served in combination with salad ingredients to make an attractive and tasty salad. The cover photograph shows lobster, prawns, Mediterranean prawns and squid mixed with curly endive [chicory], avocados and chopped cooked potato.

Salad Surprise

 ① ☒

Preparation time:
20 minutes, plus chilling time
SERVES 4

1 lb. carrots
3 rings fresh or canned pineapple
3 green eating apples
juice of 2 lemons
2 teaspoons finely chopped root ginger or preserved [candied] ginger
castor [fine] sugar

Peel and grate the carrots. Cut the pineapple into small pieces. Core and grate the apples, but do not peel them. Sprinkle with lemon juice immediately.
Mix together the carrot, pineapple, apple and root ginger. Add a little castor [fine] sugar if the apples are at at all sour.
Chill before serving.

Salad Europa

 ① ① ☒

Preparation and cooking time:
35 minutes
SERVES 4

1 lb. small new potatoes
1 clove of garlic
4 tablespoons dry white wine

freshly milled black pepper
4 oz. Italian salami, cut into ½-inch cubes
4 oz. ham cut into ½-inch cubes
4 oz. Gruyère or Emmenthal [Swiss] cheese, cut into ½ inch cubes
4 anchovy fillets, chopped
10 stuffed olives
2 tablespoons olive oil
1 tablespoon wine vinegar
To garnish:
mustard and cress or watercress

Thoroughly rinse the potatoes and cook them in boiling salted water until tender. Drain and cool.
Peel the garlic clove, cut it in half and rub the cut part over the inside of the salad bowl. Peel the potatoes and place in the bowl. Add the white wine and pepper and toss lightly.
Add the salami, ham, cheese, anchovies and olives to the potatoes. Sprinkle with the oil and vinegar and mix lightly.
Garnish with the mustard and cress or watercress.

Jellied Tomato Salad

 ① ☒ ☒

Preparation time:
30 minutes, plus 2 hours refrigeration time
SERVES 4

¼ oz. powdered gelatine
3 tablespoons water
2 tablespoons white wine vinegar
10 fl. oz. [1¼ cups] tomato juice
2 tomatoes
6 spring onions [scallions]
½ small green pepper
1 tablespoon chopped fresh parsley
To garnish:
watercress chopped
tomato slices

Gently heat the gelatine and water together until the gelatine has dissolved. Stir this and the wine vinegar into the tomato juice. Peel and chop the tomatoes and spring onions [scallions]. Core and chop the pepper. Mix all the prepared vegetables into the tomato juice and leave until it just begins to set.
Arrange a little watercress and tomato in the bottom of four small dishes or one large dish.
When the tomato juice is just

beginning to set, carefully spoon the mixture over the cress and tomato. Leave to chill in a refrigerator or a cold place until set.
Turn out on to plates and garnish with watercress and tomato slices.
Serve as a first course or with cold meats and cold fish dishes.

Saffron Rice Salad

Preparation and cooking time:
25 minutes
SERVES 4

3 oz. [½ cup] long-grain rice
¼ teaspoon saffron strands
1 red pepper
1 green pepper
12 spring onions [scallions]
4 tablespoons mango chutney
12 black olives, halved and stoned
2-3 tablespoons French Dressing
6-8 lettuce leaves, washed
4 tablespoons salted peanuts

Cover the rice with water, add the saffron strands and bring the water to the boil. Simmer for about 10 minutes or until the rice is tender. Rinse under cold running water and drain well.
De-seed and shred the peppers finely. Trim and chop the spring onions [scallions]. Chop any whole pieces of mango in the chutney. Mix the rice with the shredded peppers, onions, olives, chutney and French Dressing.
Arrange the lettuce leaves in a bowl or on a plate. Pile the rice into the centre and garnish with the peanuts.
Serve with cold meats.

Cucumber Salad

Preparation time:
40 minutes
SERVES 4-6

1 large cucumber
salt
olive oil
tarragon vinegar
To garnish:
black olives
celery leaves
1 hard-boiled egg, sliced

Slice the cucumber thinly and spread the slices out on a large plate. Sprinkle them liberally with salt and set aside for 30 minutes; the salt draws the water and indigestible juices from the cucumber.
Rinse the cucumber and drain very well.
Arrange in a bowl and sprinkle with a little olive oil and tarragon vinegar.
Garnish with black olives, celery leaves and slices of hard-boiled egg.

Tossed Green Salad

Preparation time:
30 minutes
SERVES 6

1 lettuce
1 bunch watercress
1 green pepper
6 sprigs of cauliflower
¼ medium-sized cucumber
2 shallots or small onions
1 clove of garlic
1 avocado
4 tablespoons Roquefort Dressing
freshly milled black pepper
4 tablespoons Roquefort cheese

Trim off the coarse outer leaves of the lettuce. Rinse and dry the inner leaves and shred with a stainless steel knife. Rinse and dry the watercress. De-seed and finely shred the pepper. Break the cauliflower into small pieces. Dice the cucumber. Peel and thinly slice the shallots, garlic and avocado.
Place all the prepared vegetables in a bowl, add the Roquefort Dressing and the pepper and toss well.
Crumble the Roquefort cheese over the top and serve immediately.

Variations:
A green salad makes an ideal side dish for meat or fish because it is less filling than vegetables, and it makes a pleasant contrast to a heavy main course. However, so many colourful and varied foods can be used for a salad that it is not necessary to be restricted to green alone. A platter of mixed salad is an attractive accompaniment for any cold meat or cheese. Arrange all the ingredients in a pattern, making the best use of colour so that two greens, such as lettuce and watercress, are divided by a line of

tomatoes. Use radishes, slices of hardboiled eggs, grated carrot, chicory [endive] and celery with any available cold vegetables such as peas, sweetcorn or carrots with a garnish of gherkins and olives. Serve beetroot separately because the colour will stain the rest of the salad; and spring onions [scallions] which are not popular with everyone can be bunched in a glass at the side. For any salad it is important to make as much contrast as possible in colour, taste and texture so experiment with mixtures of sweet and sour flavours, crisp and smooth ingredients.

Salad Dressings

French Dressing This is also called Vinaigrette Dressing and is the base from which many others may be made. The basic proportions are 1 part vinegar to 3 parts oil.

½ teaspoon salt
½ teaspoon freshly milled black pepper
¼ teaspoon dried mustard
2 tablespoons wine vinegar
6 tablespoons salad oil

Shake all the ingredients together in a small bottle or jar, in which the un-used dressing may be stored. Alternatively place the ingredients in a blender and mix them at the highest speed for 1 minute.

Variations:
§ *Tarragon dressing* Use tarragon vinegar instead of wine vinegar in the basic French Dressing and add 1 teaspoon of finely chopped fresh tarragon.
§ *Cumberland dressing* Prepare the French Dressing but use lemon juice instead of wine vinegar and add 1 tablespoon of redcurrant jelly and 1 tablespoon of double [heavy] cream.
§ *Roquefort dressing* Prepare the basic French dressing recipe then add 2 tablespoons crumbled Roquefort cheese and 2 teaspoons finely chopped chives or spring onion [scallion].

opposite: back: Saffron Rice Salad front: Salad Europa, Salad Surprise

JUST DESSERTS

far left: Blackberry Cream
left: Strawberry Cream Cake
below: Finnish Lemon Cake

In the summertime desserts can—and should—take advantage of the opportunities afforded by the rich supply of seasonal foods, and be concentrated on light, airy, fresh tastes rather than the substantial and filling dishes which are more appropriate to snow and sleet and dark evenings. Now is the time to serve pretty 'confections', for light whips and creams, for tart citrus-flavoured moulds, and for airy gâteaux. Since many of these desserts require no attention from you while they chill, cool, or set, you can also spend more time on decorating them, to add the final mouth-watering touches.

Charlotte Russe

Preparation time:
1 hour, plus 2-3 hours refrigeration time
S E R V E S 6

5 fl. oz. [⅝ cup] liquid lemon jelly [Jello]
6 strawberries, sliced lengthwise
angelica strips
20 sponge finger biscuits [lady fingers] or boudoir biscuits (see note)
3 egg yolks
3 tablespoons castor [fine] sugar
½ teaspoon vanilla essence
10 fl. oz. [1¼ cups] milk
¼ oz. powdered gelatine
10 fl. oz. double [1¼ cups heavy] cream, lightly whipped

Pour a little of the jelly [Jello] into a 6-inch Charlotte mould or cake tin, and leave to set. Keep the rest of the jelly warm to prevent it setting.
Make a pattern on the jelly with slices of strawberry and angelica. Very carefully spoon a little more liquid jelly over the pattern and leave until almost set. Arrange the sponge fingers upright around the sides of the mould with the ends just in the jelly. Reserve any remaining jelly.
Blend the egg yolks in a bowl with the sugar and vanilla essence.
Heat the milk to blood heat and whisk it into the egg mixture. Strain the mixture back into the pan and heat gently, stirring continuously until the mixture thickens. Do not let it boil. Set aside to cool, stirring frequently. Add more vanilla essence, if desired.
Heat the gelatine with three tablespoons of water until dissolved. Cool.
Whip half of the cream until thick.
Stir the gelatine, all the cream and any remaining lemon jelly into the egg

custard you have made, and stir until it just begins to set. Pour into the prepared mould and place in the refrigerator until set. If the Charlotte mixture does not reach the top of the biscuits, trim them down to the correct level with a sharp knife.
When the Charlotte Russe is set and ready to turn out, dip the mould into hot water for a few seconds only and then turn on to a serving dish. It is traditional to decorate this dish by tying a ribbon round the middle.

Note: the exact number of biscuits will vary according to their size and the size of the mould.

Summer Pudding

Preparation time:
45-60 minutes, plus overnight refrigeration time
S E R V E S 4-6

8 oz. blackcurrants
8 oz. bilberries [blueberries]
8 oz. raspberries
8 oz. blackberries
6 fl. oz. [¾ cup] water
6 oz. [¾ cup] sugar
1 tablespoon butter
6-8 thin slices of bread, crusts removed

Top and tail the blackcurrants and bilberries. Rinse all the fruit and place in a large saucepan with the water and sugar.
Simmer gently until all the fruit is soft. (It is not necessary to remove the seeds, but if preferred the fruit may be sieved at this stage, to make a thick purée.) Set aside to cool.
Butter a pudding bowl or soufflé mould and line it with the slices of bread. It is important not to leave any gaps in the lining.
Pour the fruit mixture into the bowl. Cover it completely with slices of bread.
Put a plate on top to fit the surface exactly and hold in place with a light weight.
Place in the refrigerator or a cool place and leave overnight. The juice from the fruit should soak through the bread.
The whole pudding can be turned out of the basin on to a plate, but it will not hold its shape indefinitely so this should be done immediately before serving. Otherwise serve the pudding from the bowl.
Serve with whipped cream.

Blackberry Cream

Preparation time:
15 minutes, plus 2-3 hours refrigeration time
S E R V E S 4

8 oz. blackberries
¼ oz. powdered gelatine
juice and grated zest of 1 lemon
10 fl. oz. double [1¼ cups heavy] cream
4 oz. castor [fine] sugar
For decoration:
whipped cream

Rinse the blackberries under cold running water and drain well. Reserve some for decoration.
Heat the gelatine in the lemon juice until thoroughly dissolved. Cool.
Whisk the cream until stiff. Add the blackberries, sugar and lemon zest and stir until well-mixed.
Stir in the dissolved gelatine and pour the mixture into a wet mould.
Place in the refrigerator for 2-3 hours.
Turn out on to a plate and decorate with whipped cream and whole blackberries.

Strawberry Cream Cake

Preparation and cooking time:
1-1½ hours
S E R V E S 6-8

2 x 6-inch plain sponge cakes (see page 62)
1 lb. strawberries
½ oz. powdered gelatine
3 tablespoons water
1 pint double [2½ cups heavy] cream
3 oz. castor [⅜ cup fine] sugar
4 oz. [1 cup] toasted flaked almonds

Cook the cakes according to the directions. Leave to cool.
Cut each sponge layer through the middle so that you have four rounds.
Place most of the strawberries in a blender and reduce to a purée. If no blender is available, mash them with a fork. Reserve some for decoration.
Heat the gelatine with the water until thoroughly dissolved. Set aside to cool.
Whip the cream and sugar together until thick. Add the strawberry purée

and gelatine and stir until the mixture begins to thicken.

Place the four layers of cake on top of one another with a thin layer of strawberry cream between each one. Coat the sides of the cake with most of the remaining strawberry cream.

Carefully transfer the cake to a serving plate and coat the sides with flaked almonds. This can be done by pressing the almonds into the cream, a few at a time, using a knife.

Cover the top with the remaining cream and decorate with halved strawberries.

Either serve immediately or keep in the refrigerator until required. It is best to serve this within 2 or 3 hours hours of preparation.

Citrus Fruit Mould

Preparation time:
5 minutes, plus overnight refrigeration time
S E R V E S 6

½ oz. powdered gelatine
juice of 3 lemons
16 fl. oz. [2 cups] fresh or canned orange juice
16 fl. oz. [2 cups] fresh or canned grapefruit juice
3 tablespoons sweet sherry
To decorate:
grapefruit segments

Heat the gelatine in the lemon juice until dissolved. Stir all the ingredients together and pour into a mould. Refrigerate overnight until set.

Turn the mould on to a plate and decorate with grapefruit segments.

Chocolate Rum Chiffon

Preparation time:
40 minutes, plus 1-2 hours refrigeration time
S E R V E S 4

4 oz. plain [semi-sweet] chocolate
4 oz. milk chocolate
2 tablespoons rum
1 tablespoon sugar
1 oz. [2 tablespoons] butter
4 eggs

5 fl. oz. double [⅝ cup heavy] cream
To decorate:
whipped cream, piped
halved walnuts

Break the chocolate into a large bowl and set aside in a saucepan of hot water until melted. Do not set it over direct heat. If the chocolate is heated too quickly it will harden.

Allow the chocolate to cool slightly and stir in the rum, sugar, butter and egg yolks.

Whip the cream lightly and stir it into the chocolate mixture.

Whisk the egg whites until very stiff and dry. Using a metal spoon, fold them into the chocolate mixture.

Pour into individual wine glasses or small dishes and refrigerate until set.

Decorate with piped whipped cream and halved walnuts.

Finnish Lemon Cake

Preparation and cooking time:
1½-2 hours
S E R V E S 6-8

1 Genoese sponge (see page 62)
3 tablespoons sugar
juice and grated zest of 2 lemons
16 fl. oz. double [2 cups heavy] cream
To decorate:
crystallized [candied] lemon slices

Cook the cake according to the directions. Leave to cool.

Heat the sugar with the lemon juice and zest until the sugar has completely dissolved. Set aside to cool.

Whip the cream until thick.

When the cake is cold, cut it into 3 rounds and sprinkle each one with the lemon syrup.

Place the rounds on a serving plate one on top of another with a layer of whipped cream between each one.

Cover the top round with the remaining cream and decorate with crystallized [candied] lemon slices.

Almond Cream Whip

Preparation time:
20 minutes, plus 1 hour refrigeration time
S E R V E S 4-6

10 fl. oz. double [1¼ cups heavy] cream
juice and grated zest of 1 small grapefruit
3 oz. castor [⅜ cup fine] sugar
1 teaspoon almond essence
2 egg whites
brandy snaps or crêpes dentelles

Place the cream, grapefruit zest, juice and sugar in a bowl. Whisk until thick. Stir in the almond essence, a drop at a time, to flavour.

Whisk the egg whites until they are very stiff and dry and fold them into the cream with a metal spoon.

Refrigerate until thick and on the point of setting.

Pile on to a serving dish and serve with brandy snaps or crêpes dentelles.

Black Cherry Meringue Flan

Preparation and cooking time:
45-60 minutes
S E R V E S 4-6

8 oz. shortcrust pastry (see page 62)
1 lb. black cherries
3 oz. [⅜ cup] granulated sugar
1 tablespoon cornflour [cornstarch]
3 tablespoons lemon juice
meringue (see page 62)

Heat the oven to 400°F (Gas Mark 6, 200°C).

Roll out the pastry and line an 8-inch flan ring.

Prick the base of the pastry with a fork and bake 'blind' in the preheated oven on the second shelf for 30 minutes.

Stone the cherries, place them in a saucepan with the sugar and lemon juice, and simmer until the cherries are soft and juicy.

Blend the cornflour [cornstarch] with a little water and add it to the cherries. Simmer, stirring continuously until the juice thickens. Pour into the pastry case.

Make the meringue following the recipe on page 62.

Pipe and pile the meringue on top of the cherries and bake in the oven for 3-4 minutes.

Serve hot or cold.

---

*opposite: back: Ice-cream with orange flavour, Almond Cream Whip
foreground: Citrus Fruit Mould*

FRESH FRUIT DESSERTS

left: Redcurrant Glory
below: Fresh Strawberries

The idea of fresh fruit is almost synonymous with that of summer. Early strawberries and raspberries served simply with thick cream; later concoctions of gooseberries and melons, apricots and plums; peaches and pineapples. Here we have selected recipes which help you make the very best of the wealth available to you. A Gooseberry Sorbet—unusual and delightful (try other fruit in the same way). A basic ice-cream which may be flavoured with any fruit juice or purée to excellent effect. And a few rather more elaborate dishes to try out as well.

Fresh Fruit

§ Certain fruits, such as apples, turn brown when cut and exposed to the air. This can be prevented by sprinkling them with lemon juice immediately.

§ Luxury fruits such as strawberries, raspberries and pineapple can be made even more luxurious if they are served sprinkled with a little Kirsch, as well as sugar and cream.

§ Oranges can be made into a delicious dessert if soaked in a mixture of brown sugar and an orange-based liqueur.

§ Strawberries sprinkled with lemon juice and sugar have an excellent flavour.

Gooseberry Sorbet

☆ ☆   ① 　 ◻ ◻

Preparation time:
20 minutes, plus 1-1½ hours refrigeration time
SERVES 4

1 lb. gooseberries
4 oz. [½ cup] sugar
5 fl. oz. [⅝ cup] water
juice and grated zest of 1 lemon
2 egg whites

Top and tail the gooseberries and rinse them under cold running water. Reserve a few gooseberries for decoration. Place the rest in a saucepan with the sugar, water, lemon juice and zest. Stew gently for 20 minutes.
Blend the stewed gooseberries to reduce them to a purée and pour into an ice tray. Place in the frozen food compartment of the refrigerator until

the mixture becomes semi-solid.
Whisk the egg whites until very stiff and fold in the gooseberry purée.
Return to the ice tray and freeze until solid.
Serve in chilled glasses with a few fresh gooseberries as decoration.

Raspberry Fool

☆   ① ①   ◻ ◻

Preparation time:
25 minutes, plus 1 hour chilling time
SERVES 4

12 oz. raspberries
4 oz. [½ cup] sugar
10 fl. oz. double [1¼ cups heavy] cream
To decorate:
whole fresh raspberries

Rinse the raspberries under cold running water then place them in a saucepan with the sugar. Heat gently until the fruit is soft.
Press the fruit through a strainer to reduce it to a purée and set aside until cold.
Whisk the cream until thick and stir three-quarters of it into the raspberry purée.
Pour into 4 small serving dishes and chill until set.
Pipe with the remaining cream and decorate with some whole raspberries.

Ice-cream Variety

☆ ☆   ①   ◻ ◻ ◻

Preparation time:
45 minutes, plus at least 2-3 hours freezing time
MAKES 1½ pints [1⅞ pints]

1 pint [2½ cups] evaporated milk or double [heavy] cream
10 fl. oz. [1¼ cups] milk
2 tablespoons custard powder
4 oz. icing [1 cup confectioners'] sugar
2-3 tablespoons vanilla essence
3 egg whites

Mix together the evaporated milk or cream and ordinary milk.
Measure the custard powder and icing [confectioners'] sugar in a bowl and

stir in the milk a little at a time. Pour into a saucepan.
Bring to the boil, stirring continuously, until the custard thickens. Remove from the heat and stir in the vanilla essence. (The mixture should be strongly flavoured, as the flavour becomes weaker when frozen.)
Pour into a bowl, cover and set aside to cool.
Pour the cold custard into a large ice tray and place in the frozen food compartment of the refrigerator until it begins to freeze around the edges.
Whisk the egg whites until stiff, then whisk in the custard very thoroughly. Return to the ice tray and place in the storage compartment until the edges begin to freeze again. Whisk thoroughly and refreeze. Repeat the whisking once more and then freeze until the ice-cream is firm enough to serve.

Variations:
§ This ice-cream can be made into a variety of flavours and colours. Omit the vanilla essence and replace it with any flavouring and colouring of your choice. The exact quantities are difficult to assess so add the colouring and flavouring a little at a time until just right. Remember to over-flavour to compensate for freezing.
§ For real fruit ice-creams, such as raspberry or blackcurrant, replace the ordinary milk with the same quantity of sweetened fruit juices, fruit purée or even stewed fruit.
§ For chocolate ice-cream, add 2 tablespoons cocoa powder to the custard powder—or coffee essence for coffee ice-cream.

Redcurrant Glory

☆ ☆   ① ①   ◻

Preparation time:
20-30 minutes
SERVES 4

12 oz. ripe redcurrants
12 oz. cream cheese
4 tablespoons castor [fine] sugar
2-3 drops vanilla essence
2 tablespoons brandy
3-4 tablespoons milk
5 fl. oz. double [⅝ cup heavy] cream
about 24 ratafia biscuits, or sponge [lady] finger biscuits

Top and tail the redcurrants. Rinse under cold running water and drain

well. Discard any berries which
are not well-ripened.
Blend the cream cheese with the
sugar and beat in the vanilla essence.
Add the brandy, a tablespoonful at a
time, and beat well.
Beat in enough of the milk to make
the mixture creamy but not soft.
Whisk the cream until thick and fold
in the cheese mixture.
Chill if necessary, until the mixture
becomes very thick.
Spoon some of the mixture into 4
individual serving glasses.
Arrange the biscuits around the sides
of the glasses and fill the centres with
redcurrants, reserving some for
decoration.
Cover with the remaining cream cheese
mixture and top with the remaining
redcurrants.
Serve immediately or refrigerate until
required. This dish can be prepared in
advance and kept overnight.

Pineapple
Surprise

Preparation time:
*30 minutes, plus 1-2 hours refrigeration
time*
S E R V E S 6

1 large pineapple
8 oz. strawberries
8 oz. raspberries
8 oz. block vanilla ice-cream
1-2 tablespoons Kirsch

Choose a pineapple with the green
spikes in good condition.
Cut right through the pineapple about
one-quarter of the way down, making
a 'base' and a 'lid'.
Scoop as much of the flesh as possible
out of the 'base' and the 'lid' and
chop it coarsely. Drain off and reserve
any excess juice for later use.
Rinse and dry the strawberries and
raspberries. Slice the strawberries.
Chill all the fruits for 1-2 hours.
Cut a very thin slice from the 'base'
of the pineapple so that it will stand
firmly on the serving dish. Place half
of the fruit in the 'base'. Cut the
ice-cream into cubes and place on top.
Cover with the remaining fruit, piling
it above the top of the 'base'. Sprinkle
with the Kirsch, and place the 'lid' on
top.
Serve immediately.

Vacharin
aux Fraises

Strawberry meringue flan

☆ ☆ ☆ ① ①   ⊠ ⊠ ⊠

Preparation and cooking time:
3-4 hours
S E R V E S 6

4 egg whites
9 oz. icing [2¼ cups confectioners']
  sugar
2 oz. [¼ cup] **finely ground hazel
  nuts**
1 tablespoon icing [confectioners']
  sugar
about 1 pint [1¼ pints] **vanilla ice-
  cream**
1 lb. strawberries
6 tablespoons raspberry jam

Heat oven to 250°F (Gas Mark ½,
130°C).
Cover a large baking tray with rice
paper. Place the egg whites in a large
bowl. Sift the icing [confectioners']
sugar and add to the egg whites.
Place the bowl over a saucepan of hot
water over low heat and whisk until a
a stiff meringue is formed.
(Alternatively, this may be done in an
electric mixer.)
Carefully fold the nuts into the
meringue.
Using a large star nozzle with a large
forcing bag, pipe a 7-8 inch ring of
meringue on to the rice paper. Fill
in the centre and then pipe two rings
on top of the outside edge to make a
basket shape. Dust very lightly with
icing [confectioners'] sugar.
Bake in the pre-heated oven for 3-4
hours. Meringue is much tastier if
it is still slightly soft in the centre so,
although the meringue should be crisp
and easy to handle, remove it from
the oven before it becomes too dry and
brittle.
Sieve the jam and add a little water
to make a thin coating syrup.
When the meringue case is cool, trim
off the excess rice paper and place
the case in a serving dish. Fill with
the ice-cream and cover with
strawberries.
Spoon the jam syrup over the
strawberries and serve immediately.

opposite: Ice-cream Variety

SUMMERTIME ENTERTAINING

As well as the menus which follow, you may like to try these, which feature recipes from the previous sections.

Peppermint Ice Grapefruit

Steak Flambé

Strawberry Cream Cake

Avgolemono Soup

Lobster Thermidor

Gooseberry Sorbet

Les Crudités

Devilled Madeira Kidneys

Summer Pudding

opposite:
It is not always possible to serve summer meals in such an elegant setting as this; but you can lay the table with your most attractive china, and decorate it with bowls of fruit and flowers, so that even a simple menu will have a taste of extravagance

The vision which may be conjured up by the subject of summertime entertaining is, surely, one of the most idyllic of romantic pictures. The lazy delight of hot sunshine, the charm of leafy green-patterned light, the promise of holidays, the scent of a host of garden flowers, the pleasures of long cool evenings following after heat-drenched days—what better way could be devised of spending such times than in the company of chosen friends? And what more appropriate method could there be of entertaining such friends, than in the relaxed and informal fashion which summer so often seems to demand?

In practice, of course, the promise offered by these expectations is often unrealized. At one time or another we have all suffered from the disappointments which attend summer with all too much frequency: 'rained-out' picnics, badly-organized barbecues with under-cooked food, wilted buffet food—as well as the more obvious hazards such as flies and mosquitoes, sun-burn, and ill-functioning air-conditioning!

Occasions to plan for

It is very clear, in fact, that our enjoyment of summer and of the entertaining we do at that time of the year is as open to interference and disruption as any other time—and so although we may wish to preserve the appearance of effortless successes, we must plan as carefully as ever against things going wrong and disrupting the enjoyment we desire. On the following pages we have planned out special menus for you to try which, with a little effort and pre-planning, will help you to avoid the more hazardous snags and pitfalls, and so leave you free to enjoy summer entertaining to the full.

Almost without exception, the sorts of occasions on which you will want to entertain in the summertime are relatively relaxed and informal ones. This is not meant to suggest that you will suddenly stop having formal dinner parties when the weather gets hot and the days longer—simply that you are less likely, in such conditions, to want to spend much time in your kitchen, and more probably will want to plan to be out of doors as much as possible. Two of the menus here are for picnics and barbecues, both of which occasions are classic summertime meals which are relaxed enough to allow for spontaneous additions of your own if you want to increase or vary the number or type of dishes. And if you do want to entertain a group of people in a rather more elaborate way we have also planned out a buffet party. This may always be adapted to suit a larger number of people, and it includes dishes which are special enough to look and taste really delicious, yet which may all be prepared ahead of time.

A Smörrebröd meal makes an excellent choice for a day-time get together—our menu, based on traditional Scandinavian dishes, could turn into a very special event without fuss or bother. Again, these dishes may all be prepared in advance, and so if you choose you may then spend your time making everything to look as it should without having to worry about the time or work to schedule. Because our menus are related to relatively informal occasions, you can adapt the dishes to be served as you choose. A picnic, for example, is an especially variable meal, for even ice-cream may be carried in a wide-topped vacuum flask, and a great variety of foods may be served whether your destination is miles away or in your own back garden. But remember that when guests are 'helping themselves', the best foods are those which come in individual portions, or which may be divided easily.

BUFFET SPREADS

opposite: back: Meringues Chantilly,
Filet de Boeuf Niçoise
foreground: Dressed Crab

This style of entertaining seems utterly ideal for the summertime, for very often the weather will be warm and fine enough to enable you to serve the food outside—perhaps on a patio, or on tables in a shady corner. If you do stay indoors however, be sure to take full advantage of the season: use a sunny and airy room to enhance the relaxed atmosphere, and if you can let the scents of summer waft in through open windows.
Table decorations may be made particularly attractive by using fresh flowers; even bought ones cost less now and the simplest arrangements look enchanting. A pretty vase with daisies; groupings of leaves and greenery; bowls of fresh fruit.

Dressed Crab

Preparation time:
1-1½ hours
SERVES 3-4

1 whole cooked crab
salt and pepper
1 hard-boiled egg, separated into
   white and yolk
paprika
lettuce leaves
mayonnaise, Rémoulade Sauce or
   French Dressing (see page 38)

Choose a crab which is not too big but feels heavy for its size. Do not buy one that smells of ammonia.
Pull off all the claws from the crab. Crack the big claws with a hammer and take out the white meat. Crack the smaller claws and pick out the meat with a skewer.
Turn the body of the crab over and remove and discard the V-shaped flap. Pull away the body of the crab and cut in half. Pick out all the white meat with a skewer.
From the inside of the crab, remove

and discard the grey fingers, any green coloured matter and any membrane which is obviously not edible.
Scoop out the brown soft meat and keep separate from the white meat. Season the meat with salt and pepper.
Pick the white meat out of the shell with a skewer and mix with the other white meat.
Press the white crab meat back into the sides of the shell. Spoon the brown meat into the centre.
Garnish with sieved egg yolk, chopped egg white and paprika.
Place on a bed of lettuce and serve with mayonnaise, Rémoulade Sauce or a French Dressing.

Filet de Boeuf Niçoise

Fillet of beef with Mediterranean vegetables

Preparation and cooking time:
2-2½ hours
SERVES 12-15

1 x 4½ lb. fillet of beef
3 tablespoons vegetable oil
2 large onions, peeled and sliced
3 cloves of garlic, peeled and sliced
2 green peppers, seeded and sliced
4 courgettes [zucchini], sliced
2 aubergines [eggplants], sliced
8 tomatoes, peeled
1 teaspoon dried basil
6 coriander seeds
salt and freshly milled black
   pepper
12 black olives, halved and stoned
5-10 fl. oz. [⅝-1¼ cups] aspic, made
   from aspic crystals

Cook the beef, following the instructions on page 23. Set aside until cold, preferably overnight.

Heat the oil in a large pan and sauté the onion and garlic until transparent. Add the green peppers, courgettes [zucchini] and aubergines [eggplants] and cook very slowly until they begin to soften and exude water.
Add the tomatoes, basil, coriander, salt and pepper. Cover and simmer until all the vegetables are tender.
Add the black olives and set aside until cold. Drain off any excess liquid.
Thinly slice the beef and arrange on a large flat plate. Carefully spoon over the aspic and leave until set. The aspic is used only to prevent the meat from drying and only the thinnest covering is necessary.
Garnish the meat with some of the stewed vegetables and serve the rest separately.

Meringues Chantilly

Preparation and cooking time:
2½ hours
MAKES 9-12 MERINGUES

1 teaspoon olive oil
meringue mixture (see page 62)
8 fl. oz. double [1 cup heavy] cream
1 tablespoon castor [fine] sugar
¼-½ teaspoon vanilla essence

Heat the oven to 225°F (Gas Mark ¼, 110°C).
Lightly grease a large baking tray with olive oil.
Using a forcing bag and a ½-inch plain nozzle, pipe the meringue on to the greased baking tray in small shell shapes.
Place the meringues on the bottom shelf of the preheated oven for 1½-2 hours. The meringues should now be dry and crisp on the outside and soft inside; and they will probably have turned a very pale coffee colour. (To have really white meringues leave the oven door ajar and bake for at least 3-4 hours.) When the meringues are dry enough, they will lift off the baking tray without difficulty. Cool on a wire tray.
Whip the cream with the sugar and vanilla essence until thick enough to pipe.
Sandwich two meringues together with piped cream.
Serve as soon as possible, or the plain meringues can be stored in an airtight tin for at least a week.

BARBECUE DISHES

Two examples of the variety of foods
suitable for barbecue cooking.

These can be tremendous fun, and a wonderfully friendly way of entertaining your family or your friends. Many people now have barbecue kits for their gardens— and others are intrepid enough to set up barbecue arrangements at holiday spots on beaches, or in the country.

These four recipes would make excellent choices for this essentially casual style of eating. All are main dishes—fresh fruit can follow; and a salad with rolls and butter are the only accompaniments necessary, although if you are at home you could provide more elaborate ones. Jacket potatoes are always welcome and may easily be wrapped in foil and tucked among the ashes in the fire.

Frankfurters with Barbecue Sauce

Preparation time:
40 minutes
SERVES 4

5 tablespoons water
5 tablespoons sugar
2 tablespoons malt vinegar
2 tablespoons Worcestershire sauce
4 tablespoons lemon juice
5 fl. oz. [⅝ cup] beef stock
1 large onion
5 fl. oz. [⅝ cup] tomato ketchup
1 tablespoon cornflour [cornstarch]
dash Tabasco sauce
8 small frankfurters

Heat the water and sugar over low heat until the sugar dissolves. Increase the heat and boil rapidly until the liquid becomes a thick golden-brown syrup.
Remove from the heat and immediately add the vinegar, Worcestershire sauce, lemon juice and stock. The mixture will bubble furiously at this stage and the syrup will solidify. Heat slowly until this melts.
Peel and chop the onion and add to the sauce. Simmer for 20 minutes or until the onion is tender.
Blend the cornflour [cornstarch] with a little cold water and stir this into the sauce. Add the Tabasco. Stir until the sauce thickens.
Add the frankfurters and simmer for 5 minutes.
The sauce and frankfurters can be kept

hot over the barbecue. If the sauce thickens too much, thin it down with water.

Spatchcock of Chicken

Preparation and cooking time:
45 minutes, plus 1 hour marinating time
SERVES 2-4

1 x 3 lb. chicken
3 tablespoons lemon juice
½ teaspoon salt
1½ oz. [3 tablespoons] melted butter

Cut the chicken along the back bone and force open until flat. Press two long metal skewers into the drumstick on one side, through the breast and out of the drumstick on the other side. This will hold the chicken in shape during grilling [broiling] and can be used to turn the chicken over.
Sprinkle with lemon juice and salt and set aside for 1 hour. Brush the chicken with melted butter and grill [broil] over the barbecue for about 15 minutes on the bony side. Turn over and grill [broil] for about 15 minutes on the other side. The exact time will depend on the intensity of heat from the fire.
Serve with baked potatoes or crusty bread and different kinds of chutney.

Spare Ribs of Pork

Preparation time:
10 minutes, plus 1 hour marinating time
SERVES 6-8

3 lb. spare ribs of pork
1 large onion
3 tablespoons sesame oil (see page 26)
3 fl. oz. [⅜ cup] soy sauce

Separate the ribs with a sharp knife.
Peel and grate the onion and place in a large bowl with the sesame oil and

soy sauce. Add the ribs a few at a time, turning them over several times to coat them in the marinade.
Set aside to marinate for at least 1 hour, turning the spare ribs frequently.
Grill [broil] over the barbecue until brown and crisp. Brush them frequently during cooking with the marinade.
Serve with any spicy sauce.

Trout Parcels

Preparation and cooking time:
40-45 minutes
SERVES 6

As an alternative to the usual way of cooking meat and fish on a grill or spit over a barbecue, the food can be wrapped in aluminium foil parcels. The advantages of this method are numerous:
1. The hostess can prepare all the parcels in advance.
2. While cooking, the food needs little attention. Constant basting and turning is unnecessary.
3. Each guest can open a parcel and use the foil as a plate, thus eliminating the need for serving plates and washing up.
4. The natural flavours from the food are not wasted in the fire but rather sealed in by the foil.
The following recipe is an example of a dish that can be cooked in foil with delicious results.

6 rainbow or blue trout
6 sprigs fresh thyme
3 oz. [6 tablespoons] butter
3 lemons
salt and pepper
6 x 12 inch squares aluminium foil

Gut the trout and rinse well.
Put a sprig of thyme and ½ oz. [1 tablespoon] butter inside each trout.
Place each trout on a square of foil and sprinkle with the juice of half a lemon and salt and pepper.
Wrap the foil around each trout, taking care not to leave any openings.
Place in the hot coals and cook for about 30 minutes, turning once.

Variation: Use chicken drum sticks with finely shredded green pepper, finely chopped onion, salt and pepper and ½ oz. [1 tablespoon] of butter. Increase the cooking time to about 1 hour.

A SMÖRREBRÖD MEAL

opposite: Open Sandwiches

The Danes' word for their open sandwiches translates simply as 'buttered bread'—yet how different they are from the usual sandwich. In a true display of this food attention is always paid to composing an arrangement of colour, texture and flavour —and all planned with as much care as a painting for a truly classic effect. They are of course also very filling: three or four pieces of smörrebröd make a filling and satisfying course.

Try this authentic sample of the Scandinavian menu's wonderful flavours. A range of open sandwiches; salmon marinated in a dill mixture—and to finish a delicious thickened 'fruit purée', served with cream.

Open Sandwiches

 ① ①

Preparation time:
2-3 minutes for each sandwich

For the base of all the following open sandwiches use slices of rye bread, spread with unsalted butter.
§ *Cover* the bread with a slice of smoked salmon. Top with a lettuce leaf, three or four prawns or shrimps, a teaspoon of mayonnaise and a twist of lemon.
§ *Cover* the bread with slices of Danish blue cheese. Top with very thin onion rings, wedges of tomato and a sprig of parsley. Sprinkle lightly with French dressing.
§ *Roll* a slice of ham into a cone and place diagonally on the bread. Put slices of gherkin and slices of stuffed olives either side and stuff the ham cone with chopped watercress tossed in French Dressing.
§ *Cover* the bread with a slice of roast chicken. Top with slices of hard-boiled egg and dress with a teaspoon of curried mayonnaise.

§ *Cover* the bread with a slice of roast pork. Top with slices of beetroot [beet] and a mixture of finely chopped onion and parsley.
§ *Cover* the bread with a lettuce leaf. Top with a tablespoon of potato salad, a slice of salted herring and slices of cucumber and tomato.

Dill-cured Salmon

  ① ① ①

Preparation time:
30 minutes, plus 24 hours refrigeration time
SERVES 8-10

2 lb. middle cut of salmon
2 tablespoons castor [fine] sugar
2 tablespoons coarse salt
1 large bunch fresh dill
8 white peppercorns, cracked
To garnish:
lemon wedges

Cut the salmon through the bone to make two flat steaks. Remove the bones, taking care not to pull away the flesh.
Rub the salmon all over with a mixture of salt and sugar.
Rinse the dill thoroughly under cold running water and dry well.
Place one half of the salmon on a board. Cover with the dill and sprinkle with the peppercorns. Place the other half on top, thick end to thin end. Cover with a plate or board with a heavy weight on top.
Refrigerate for at least 24 hours. The salmon will then be 'cured' enough to eat. It will keep for 2-3 days in the refrigerator but not indefinitely.
Cut the salmon into very thin slices and remove the skin. Arrange the slices on a serving dish and garnish with lemon wedges.

Dill Sauce

 ①

Preparation time:
10-15 minutes
SERVES 4

1 tablespoon mild French mustard
1 tablespoon hot Dijon mustard
1 tablespoon castor [fine] sugar
2 tablespoons white wine vinegar
2 tablespoons vegetable oil
4 tablespoons chopped dill
¼ teaspoon salt
¼ teaspoon freshly milled black pepper

Blend the mustards, sugar, salt, pepper and vinegar in a small bowl.
Beat in the oil, drop by drop.
Adjust the seasoning, if necessary.
Stir in the dill.
Serve with Dill-cured Salmon (above).

Rödgröd med Flöde
Scandinavian fruit purée

 ① ①

Preparation and cooking time:
40 minutes
SERVES 4-6

8 oz. redcurrants
8 oz. raspberries
8 oz. rhubarb
1¼ pints [3 cups] water
6 oz. [¾ cup] sugar
2 tablespoons cornflour [cornstarch]

Rinse the redcurrants and raspberries under cold running water. Drain and place in a large saucepan. Rinse and chop the rhubarb and add to the saucepan, together with the water and sugar. Simmer very gently until all the fruit is soft.
Strain, reserving the juice only (the fruit can be used for other dishes such as trifles or with ice-cream).
Blend the cornflour [cornstarch] in the saucepan with 2-3 tablespoons cold water. Add the fruit juice. Return to the heat and bring to the boil, stirring continuously until the mixture thickens.
Cool, stirring frequently to prevent a skin forming.
Serve either warm or completely cold, with single [light] cream.

PICNIC PARTIES

left: Curd Cheese Sandwich
below: Make the occasion special by
leaving the plastic plates behind, and
producing picnic food in a grand way.

Picnics tend to be of two very distinct types: those which are spontaneous and quickly-arranged meals, stemming perhaps from a simple wish to eat out-of-doors in sunny weather—and those which are planned with the precision of military operations with nothing left to chance (except the weather). Whether you're a plan-ahead or a free-and-easy picnicker, we think you'll find these recipes ideal for the occasion. All four may be made up ahead of time, are light and summery, yet filling enough to satisfy out-door hunger pangs. The Curd Cheese Sandwich is particularly unusual, and deliciously tasty.

Curd Cheese Sandwich

Preparation time:
10 minutes
SERVES 6-8

1 large round brown or white loaf
2 oz. [4 tablespoons] butter
4 slices ham
4 tomatoes
1 lb. curd cheese or cream cheese
chopped parsley

Cut three ½ inch thick slices of bread.
Spread one slice with butter and cover with ham. Spread both sides of the second slice with butter and place on top of the ham. Cover this with slices of tomato. Spread one side of the third slice of bread with butter and place on the tomatoes, buttered side down.
Cover top and sides completely with curd cheese and sprinkle with chopped parsley.
Chill well before taking on a picnic.

Quiche Breton
Bacon, egg and onion flan

Preparation and cooking time:
1 hour
SERVES 6

8 oz. rich short crust pastry (see page 62)
6 slices streaky bacon
2 eggs
8 fl. oz. single [1 cup light] cream
2 teaspoons finely chopped onion
2 teaspoons finely chopped parsley
3 oz. [¾ cup] grated Gruyère or Emmental [Swiss] cheese

Heat oven to 400°F (Gas Mark 6, 200°C).
Roll out the pastry and line an 8-9 inch flan tin. Prick the bottom of the flan case lightly with a fork and bake 'blind' on the top shelf of the oven for 20 minutes.
Cut the rind from the bacon and grill [broil] until crisp. Cool.
Whisk the eggs with the cream. Add the onion and the parsley and mix well.
Place the slices of bacon in the flan case and pour over the egg mixture. Sprinkle with the grated cheese.
Lower the temperature of the oven to 375°F (Gas Mark 5, 190°C) and bake on the top shelf for 20 minutes or until set and golden brown.
Serve cold with salads.

Huntsman's Pork Pie

Preparation and cooking time:
3 hours
SERVES 6

For the hot water crust pastry
10 oz. [2½ cups] plain [all-purpose] flour
½ teaspoon salt
1 egg yolk
3 oz. [⅜ cup] lard or vegetable shortening
5 fl. oz. [⅝ cup] water
For the filling
1½ lb pork—fat and lean, diced
¼ teaspoon salt
¼ teaspoon freshly milled black pepper
¼ teaspoon dried sage
10 fl. oz. [1¼ cups] chicken stock
½ oz. gelatine
1 egg white

Heat the oven to 400°F (Gas Mark 6, 200°C).
To make the pastry, sift the flour and salt into a bowl. Make a well in the centre and drop in the egg yolk.
Heat the lard or vegetable shortening and water together until boiling. Pour this mixture into the flour and start beating immediately with a wooden spoon.
Continue beating until the pastry is smooth and cool enough to handle.

Knead the pastry on a smooth surface until pliable and no longer sticky. Cover and allow to rest for 15 minutes.
Take two-thirds of the pastry and roll it out into a circle with a 12-inch diameter. Set the remaining one third of the pastry aside for later use.
Take a large jar, about 5 inches in diameter, flour it and turn it upside down. Mould the rolled-out pastry around the upturned base of the jar, making a pie case 3-4 inches deep. Wrap a double sheet of greaseproof [waxed] paper completely around the pastry and tie it in position with string.
Turn upright and set aside until the pie case is firm.
Twist the jar out of the pastry and fill the pie case with the pork. Sprinkle with salt, pepper and sage, and add 3 tablespoons of the stock.
Roll out the remaining pastry to fit the top of the pie. Place on top of the meat and squeeze the 2 layers of pastry together. Make a small hole in the centre of the pie and brush the top with egg white.
Place on a baking sheet and bake on the middle shelf of the preheated oven for 30 minutes. Lower the heat to 350°F (Gas Mark 4, 180°C) and bake for a further 1½ hours. Cool.
Dissolve the gelatine in the stock. Allow to cool and pour the mixture into the pie. Leave the pie in a cold place until set.

Romany Cakes

Preparation time:
25 minutes
SERVES 6

3 oz. full fat soft cheese
5 oz. cottage cheese
3 oz. castor [⅜ cup fine] sugar
juice of 1 lemon
5 fl. oz. double [⅝ cup heavy] cream
6 digestive biscuits [Graham crackers]
6 teaspoons apricot jam
6 small pineapple rings

Blend together the cheeses and sugar. Stir in the lemon juice and cream and place in the refrigerator until it begins to thicken.
Crush the digestive biscuits [graham crackers] to crumbs and mix with the jam. Spoon this mixture into 6 paper trifle [cup cake] cases and place a pineapple ring on top of each.
When the cheese mixture is thick, pour over the pineapple rings. Refrigerate until set.

ICY THIRST ~ QUENCHERS

The more active life most of us lead in summer, combined with the effects of the warm weather, make interesting and refreshing drinks a necessity. Here we suggest ways in which to make a variety of thirst-quenchers. Two are alcoholic; the others right for all ages. Try the punch and the sparkling wine cup at a buffet party, before Sunday lunch, or in the late afternoon with a light snack. There's a rich and satisfying Iced Coffee, an unusual way of serving tea in the Citrus Cup—and a delightfully pretty Californian Cocktail, with all the tastes of summer.

Sangria

Preparation time:
5 minutes
SERVES 6-8

1 pint 6 fl. oz. [3¼ cups] **Spanish red wine**
1 pint [2½ cups] **lemonade**
4 tablespoons **brandy**
1 **orange**, sliced
2 **limes**, sliced
2 **lemons**, sliced
2-3 **cloves**
20-24 **ice cubes**

Pour the wine, lemonade and brandy into a jug. Add slices of orange, lime. and lemon, the cloves and ice cubes.
Stir and serve immediately.

Pineapple Punch

Preparation time:
5 minutes, plus 1 hour refrigeration time
SERVES 8-12

1 pint [2½ cups] **pineapple juice**
½ bottle [13 fl. oz.] **dry white wine**
10 fl. oz. [1¼ cups] **orange juice**
3-4 tablespoons **brandy**
soda water
To garnish:
grapes
sliced mixed fruit of your choice

Pour the fruit juices, white wine and brandy into a large jug. Mix and chill well.
Add soda water to taste just before serving.
Garnish with grapes and slices of other fruits.

Iced Coffee

Preparation time:
10 minutes, plus 30-40 minutes refrigeration time
SERVES 3-4

1 **vanilla pod**
1 pint [2½ cups] **very hot strong black coffee**
4 oz. castor [½ cup fine] **sugar**
10 fl. oz. [1¼ cups] **hot milk**
5 tablespoons double [heavy] **cream**

Add the vanilla pod and castor [fine] sugar to the coffee and stir well.
Stir in the milk and taste. Add more sugar if necessary.
Chill the coffee completely, in the refrigerator, stirring and tasting occasionally. Remove the vanilla pod when the flavour is strong enough.
Pour into ice trays and place in a frozen food compartment until semi-solid.
Pour back into a pitcher, stir with a fork until liquid again and whisk in the double [heavy] cream.
Serve immediately in tall glasses.

California Cocktail

Preparation time:
5 minutes
SERVES 2

10 fl. oz. [1¼ cups] **orange juice**
10 fl. oz. [1¼ cups] **apple juice**
10 fl. oz. [1¼ cups] **grape juice**
juice of 1 grapefruit
juice of 2 lemons
3-4 tablespoons **crushed ice**

2 tablespoons **sultanas or raisins**
1 **red eating apple**, cored and sliced
soda water

Pour all the juices into a large pitcher and add the ice, sultanas or raisins and slices of apple.
Stir well and pour into glasses.
Add a dash of soda water just before serving.

Sparkling White Wine Cup

Preparation time:
5 minutes
SERVES 8-12

12 **ice-cubes**
1 ice-cold bottle [26 fl. oz.] **sparkling white wine**
2 fl. oz. [¼ cup] **Curaçao**
6 fl. oz. [¾ cup] **brandy**
10 fl. oz. [1¼ cups] **orange juice**
1 pint [2½ cups] ice-cold **soda water**
slices of cucumber skin
a few strawberries
2-3 **sprigs mint**

Put the ice-cubes in a large pitcher and add all the ingredients.
Stir well and serve immediately.

Citrus Tea Cup

Preparation and cooking time:
1 hour 10 minutes
SERVES 3-4

1½ pints [3¾ cups] **freshly made China tea**
thinly pared zest of 1 orange
1 **thinly sliced lemon**
1 **clove**
¼ inch **cinnamon stick**
2 teaspoons **rose-water** (optional)

Heat together all the ingredients until hot but not boiling.
Set aside to cool and infuse. Strain.
Reheat when required and add honey and sugar to taste.
Serve in tall glasses with a slice of orange or lemon.

---

opposite: Pineapple Punch

BASIC RECIPES

Puff Pastry

Preparation time:
1 hour, plus 2½ hours resting time
MAKES 8 oz.

8 oz. [2 cups] flour
½ teaspoon salt
2 teaspoons lemon juice
7-8 tablespoons cold water
4 oz. [½ cup] margarine
4 oz. [½ cup] vegetable fat

Sift the flour and salt into a medium-sized mixing bowl. Make a well in the centre and add the lemon juice and 6 tablespoons of the water. Mix to a soft dough with a table knife. Add the remaining water, if necessary.
Knead the dough well on a lightly floured surface until it is smooth and elastic. Wrap in aluminium foil and set aside in a cool place for at least 30 minutes to rest.
Meanwhile blend the margarine and vegetable fat together and re-shape into an oblong about 5 by 4 inches.
Roll the dough into an oblong, about 15 by 5 inches. Place the fat lengthwise in the centre. Fold the pastry over the fat from both sides, making a square. Seal the edges together by tapping lightly with a rolling pin to enclose the fat completely. Turn the square once in a clockwise direction so that the edge furthest away becomes the right-hand edge.
Roll the dough again into an oblong. Fold the bottom third up and the top third down to make a square as before. Seal the edges.
Turn the square once in a clockwise direction so that the edge furthest away becomes the right-hand edge. Wrap the dough in aluminium foil and leave it in a cool place for 30 minutes.
Repeat the process of rolling, folding and turning the dough six more times setting it aside to rest after the 4th,

6th and 8th rollings. These rest periods are most important and must not be omitted. If they are, the pastry will become sticky and elastic and will be very difficult to roll.
When the pastry has rested after the final rolling, use as required. Providing the pastry is covered with foil or plastic film wrap it can be kept for 2 or 3 days.

Batter

Preparation time:
20 minutes
MAKES 10 fl. oz. [1¼ cups]

4 oz. [1 cup] flour
½ teaspoon salt
2 eggs
1 tablespoon melted butter
8 fl. oz. [1 cup] brown ale

Sift the flour and salt into a medium-sized mixing bowl and make a well in the centre. Add the egg, the melted butter and a little of the brown ale. Mix well with a wooden spoon. Add half of the remaining brown ale and beat well for 3-4 minutes. Stir in the remaining ale and beat lightly. Set aside for at least 15 minutes.
Use as required.
This mixture can be stored in the refrigerator for up to 2 days.

Béchamel Sauce

Preparation and cooking time:
20 minutes
MAKES 10 fl. oz. [1¼ cups]

1 small onion, peeled
1 small carrot, peeled
10 fl. oz. [1¼ cups] milk
1 blade or ¼ teaspoon ground mace
1 small bay leaf
4 peppercorns
2 cloves
1 oz. [2 tablespoons] butter

3 tablespoons flour

Place the onion and carrot in a saucepan with the milk, mace, bay leaf, peppercorns and cloves. Bring to the boil then remove from the heat, cover and set aside to infuse for about 15 minutes. Strain.
Melt the butter in a saucepan. Stir in the flour and cook gently for 30 seconds. Remove from the heat and add the infused milk a little at a time, mixing well between each addition. Bring to the boil, stirring continuously until the mixture thickens. Use as required.

Mayonnaise

Preparation time:
30 minutes
MAKES 10 fl. oz. [1¼ cups]

2 egg yolks
1 teaspoon salt
1 teaspoon white pepper
1 teaspoon castor [fine] sugar
1 teaspoon French mustard
2 teaspoons lemon juice
10 fl. oz. [1¼ cups] olive oil
about 2 tablespoons white wine
   vinegar

Blend the egg yolks with the seasonings and lemon juice in a round-bottomed bowl. Beat with a small wire whisk or wooden spoon for 2-3 minutes until slightly thickened.
Start adding the oil 2 or 3 drops at a time, beating very thoroughly between each addition. When half of the oil has been added, the mayonnaise should be very thick. Continue adding the oil and beating well. The amount added each time can be increased until finally the last quarter of the oil can be added in a steady stream.
When all the oil has been added, stir in the vinegar. The quantity may be increased or decreased, according to

the sharpness of flavour required.
Store in a cool place.

Variations:
§ *Curry Mayonnaise:* Add 4 teaspoons of curry powder with the seasonings and stir in a little sweetened apricot purée or apricot chutney to taste, once all the oil has been added. Serve with cold chicken and fish dishes.
§ *Mayonnaise sauce for prawn or shrimp cocktail:* Add 2-3 tablespoons tomato purée, 1 tablespoon lemon juice and Tabasco sauce to taste when all the oil has been added.
§ *Rémoulade sauce:* Add 2 teaspoons Dijon mustard, 1 teaspoon anchovy essence, 1 tablespoon mixed chopped gherkins and capers and 1 teaspoon mixed chopped parsley and tarragon. Mix well and serve with fried or grilled [broiled] fish, and grilled [broiled] or roasted meats.

Meringue

Preparation time:
5 minutes

2 egg whites
4 oz. castor [½ cup fine] sugar

Place the egg whites in a large bowl. Whisk until they are stiff and dry and will stand in firm peaks.
Add half of the sugar and whisk until as stiff as before. Fold in the remaining sugar with a metal spoon.
Use the meringue as soon as possible, as it will separate if kept too long.

Genoese Sponge

Preparation time:
15 minutes
MAKES 1 deep 8″ cake or
    2 shallow 6″ cakes

4 large eggs
4 oz. castor [½ cup fine] sugar
4 oz. [1 cup] flour
4 tablespoons melted butter

Heat the oven to 375°F (Gas Mark 5, 190° C).
Break the eggs into a medium-sized mixing bowl and add the sugar. Stand the bowl over a saucepan of hot water and whisk the eggs and sugar until they become very thick and white. The mixture should be thick enough to leave a trail.
Sift the flour on to the mixture. Pour the melted butter down the side and fold in very gently, using a metal spoon.
Pour the sponge mixture into the greased tins and bake in the preheated oven. For an 8-inch deep cake cook on the middle shelf for 1 hour. For 2 shallow 6-inch cakes cook on the second shelf down for 35-40 minutes.
When the cakes are firm to the touch, turn on to a wire rack and leave to cool.

Rich Short Crust Pastry

Preparation time:
10 minutes
MAKES 8 oz.

8 oz. [2 cups] flour
pinch of salt
3 oz. [⅜ cup] margarine
2 oz. [¼ cup] vegetable fat
2 tablespoons cold water

Sift the flour and salt into a medium-sized mixing bowl. Cut the margarine and vegetable fat into small pieces and using your fingertips rub the fats into the flour until the mixture resembles fine breadcrumbs. Add the water to the flour mixture and mix it to a firm dough.
Knead until smooth, on a lightly floured surface, but avoid overhandling.
Use as required. To store, wrap in aluminium foil and refrigerate.

CARVING MEAT & PREPARING FISH

1. Leg of Lamb
Remove two or three thick slices as shown, and continue cutting down to the bone taking further slices from either side of the first one. Turn the joint over and cut flat slices along
the leg on the under side.
2. Chicken or Turkey
Remove the drumsticks, carving the meat off in slices if the joints are large enough. Cut the breast in thin slices from both sides of
the breast bone, and serve this white meat with some dark meat sliced from the thighs.
3. Duck
If it is a large bird the legs are removed and served as two portions.

GLOSSARY OF COOKERY TERMS

Bain marie
A baking tin half filled with hot water in which custards and pâtés are cooked. It can also be used for keeping food warm.

To bake blind
To bake a flan or pie case without filling. To prevent the sides from falling, line pastry case with greaseproof [waxed] paper and fill with dried beans or uncooked rice.

To baste
To spoon fat or liquid over food (usually meat or fish) during cooking, to keep it moist.

To blanch
To whiten some meats, such as sweetbreads and tripe, by putting into cold water and bringing to the boil.
To remove the skins of almonds or tomatoes, by putting into boiling water.
To partly cook some vegetables or fruit, for example peppers or oranges, to reduce the sharp taste.

Bouquet garni
4 sprigs of parsley, 1 sprig of thyme and a small bay leaf tied in a piece of muslin. Made-up sachets of bouquet garnis are now easily obtained.

To coat
To cover food completely before cooking: i.e. with egg and breadcrumbs, batter, etc.
Food may be coated after cooking, with a sauce or icing.

Croûtons
Small pieces of fried or toasted bread, used to garnish—or serve with—soups and other dishes.

To curdle
The ingredients separate instead of combining—often through over-heating, or through adding one ingredient too fast.

To dice
To cut into even pieces. Slice the food, cut the slices into strips, and then into cubes.

To dredge
To coat lightly with flour or sugar.

To flake
A term generally used with fish; meaning to divide into small pieces, with a fork.

To fold in
To cut ingredients gently together so that as much air as possible is trapped within the mixture.

To glaze
To give a shine.
Pastry is brushed with beaten egg before baking, or fruit with sieved apricot jam.

To marinate
To steep meat, fish or vegetables in a liquid containing acid, usually in the form of wine and lemon juice, which gives flavour and helps to tenderize meat. The liquid is known as a marinade.

To pare
To remove skin or zest.

Remove the wishbone and cut the duck in half down the centre as shown. Carve the breast in slices, and serve the meat from one side, together with the wing, as a portion. If the bird is small simply divide it in half as before, but serve each complete side as a portion.

4. Filleting a flat fish
Cut down the centre of the fish, and insert a sharp knife under the flesh on the backbone. Working towards the fins cut the fillet clear of the bone, and repeat this on both sides of the fish so that you have four fillets.

To poach
To cook slowly in liquid, which is just simmering, *not* boiling.

To purée
To put through a sieve, or into a blender, to achieve a smooth mixture.

Roux
A mixture of fat and flour used as the base for many sauces.

To rub in
To rub fat into flour with the fingertips until it looks like fine breadcrumbs.

To sauté
To cook in hot fat, tossing frequently.

To simmer
To cook, *below* boiling point.

Zest
The thin coloured part of the skin of an orange or lemon. Remove it with a very fine grater or gently rub a sugar cube over the surface to absorb the oil.

below: Prepare ahead and enjoy a picnic lunch. Use foil dishes, vacuum flasks, or even a handy serving dish to pack the food —and don't forget the salt and pepper.

General Trading Company
144 Sloane Street London SW1

Habitat
Fulham Road London SW7

Harrods Limited
Knightsbridge London SW3

Harvey Nichols
Sloane Street London SW1

James Hardy & Company
235 Brompton Road London SW3

Pugh and Carr
126 Knightsbridge London SW3

Reject China Shop
36a Beauchamp Place London SW3

The Warehouse
29 Neal Street London WC2

Photographs by:
Bryce Attwell; pages 6, 9, 10 (bottom
picture), 13 14, 27, 28 (bottom picture),
31, 32 (bottom picture), 39, 51, 55, 60
Camera Press; pages 4, 10 (top
picture), 17, 18, 21, 22, 28 (top
picture), 32 (top picture), 35, 40, 44,
47, 48, 52, 56, 59, 64
DELU/PAF International; page 36
Syndication International; page 1
ZEFA; pages 25, 43

We should like to thank the following
companies for their help in supplying
accessories for photography.

Casa Pupo Tile Shop
Pimlico Road London SW1

David Mellor
4 Sloane Square London SW1

Elizabeth David
46 Bourne Street London SW1

Recipes and preparation of food for
photography by Gwyneth Loveday
Illustrations by Susan Richards

Important

Readers please note: Equivalents for American ingredients are given in the text in square brackets.

All weight and measure equivalents are approximate.
Tablespoons and teaspoons are Standard Spoon measures and are level.

Key to Symbols

☆ This is a guide to each recipe's preparation and cooking

☆ Easy

☆ ☆ Requires special care

☆ ☆ ☆ Complicated

① This is a guide to the cost of each dish and will, of course, vary according to region and season

① Inexpensive

① ① Reasonable

① ① ① Expensive

⧖ This is a guide to the preparation and cooking time required for each dish and will vary according to the skill of the individual cook

⧖ Less then 1 hour

⧖ ⧖ Between 1 hour and 2½ hours

⧖ ⧖ ⧖ Over 2½ hours

Equivalents

Dry measures

Metric	Imperial and American
28.3 grams (approx. 30 grams)	1 oz.
85 grams	3 oz.
454 grams (approx. 500 grams or ½ kg.)	1 lb. (16 oz.)
1000 grams or 1 kg.	35 oz. (2 lb. 3 oz.)

Liquid measures

Metric	Imperial	American
5 ml. approx.	⅙ fl. oz.	1 teaspoon
15 ml. approx.	½ fl. oz.	1 tablespoon
30 ml. approx.	1 fl. oz.	2 tablespoons
2.27 dl.	8 fl. oz.	1 cup
2.83 dl.	10 fl. oz. (½ pint)	1½ cups
4.5 dl. or .45 litre (approx. ½ litre)	16 fl. oz.	1 pint (2 cups)
5.68 dl.	20 fl. oz. (1 pint)	2½ cups
10 dl. or 1 litre	35 fl. oz. (2 lb. 3 oz.)	4⅓ cups